= *The* =

ECKERT FAMILY
FALL COOKBOOK

APPLE, PUMPKIN, SQUASH RECIPES & MORE

SEVEN GENERATIONS OF RECIPES FROM OUR ORCHARD

REEDY PRESS
St. Louis, Missouri

Reedy Press
PO Box 5131
St. Louis, MO 63139, USA

Library of Congress Control Number: 2012947020

ISBN: 978-1-935806-36-3

Please visit our website at www.reedypress.com.

Design by Matt Johnson

Printed in the United States of America
12 13 14 15 16   5 4 3 2 1

CONTENTS

INTRODUCTION

So many things excite us about the fall season on the farm. Generation after generation, our family anxiously anticipates the crisp fall air, the shorter days, the sweet smell of ripening apples and new flavors around our dinner tables. *The Eckert Family Fall Cookbook* is our way of sharing the best of the fall season's bountiful harvest with you.

Food preparation—as well as consumption!—is a great way to bring families together. We have so many memories of family time spent around the dinner table—telling stories, laughing, and sometimes even a competition of whose dessert recipe was better.

We are passionate about the fruits we grow at Eckert's and love to experiment with new flavors and combinations, but we also respect the experience and knowledge of those who came before us. Several recipes in this volume were handed down from our grandmothers, who were unbelievably good cooks and bakers. Some recipes had to be tweaked for modern-day baking, but they are traditional nonetheless. Other recipes came from cooking classes in our classroom where we love to experiment with new techniques in a modern-day kitchen.

When deciding what to prepare for a meal, begin with the freshest, unprocessed ingredients of the season. As our grandmothers taught us, the closer you can get to where the product was grown, the better it will taste. Most fruits and vegetables don't need heavy seasonings or extra spices to make them taste good. Fresh ingredients speak for themselves.

Each season brings a different bounty to the kitchen. We began our seasonal series of cookbooks in the fall because apples have been a staple of the Eckert's farms for more than 100 years. The harvest of the fall season is very versatile. We hope this book will help you to treasure traditional recipes as well as stretch you into trying something new.

Eat fresh, eat by the season, and enjoy sharing the fruits of your labor.

SNACKS, SALADS, & SOUPS

— *From Our Family Album* —

For seven generations the Eckert family has been raising fruit in St. Clair County, Illinois. Each generation has passed on its knowledge and experience and has helped nurture the forthcoming generation. Alvin Eckert and his son, Vernon, are pictured here in 1935. They are working in an apple orchard in Belleville. Alvin is showing Vernon how to graft new bud wood onto existing trees.

Baked Blue and Brie Cheese with Apple Wedges

1 wedge (8 oz.) Brie cheese
¼ cup crumbled blue cheese
Apple wedges

Preheat oven to 350°F. Cut Brie horizontally in half. Place bottom half, cut-side up, in small ovenproof dish. Sprinkle blue cheese over Brie; top with top half of Brie, cut-side down. Bake 5 minutes or until cheeses are slightly softened. (Do not overbake or cheeses will become runny.) Serve immediately as a spread with the apple wedges.

Apple Nachos

3 apples, cored, cut into ¼-inch slices
1 to 2 Tbs. caramel sauce
1 to 2 Tbs. chocolate sauce
1 Tbs. peanuts, chopped
1 Tbs. mini chocolate chips
1 Tbs. sprinkles (optional)

Arrange apples on serving plate. Drizzle with caramel and chocolate sauces. Sprinkle with nuts, chocolate chips, and sprinkles. Serve immediately.

Toasted Squash or Pumpkin Seeds

Squash seeds and/or pumpkin seeds
Vegetable oil
Salt, to taste

Preheat oven to 325°F. Rinse seeds well; dry thoroughly. Toss seeds with enough vegetable oil to coat lightly; salt to taste. Arrange seeds in single layer in shallow baking pan. Bake 10 to 15 minutes or until seeds are crisp, stirring after 5 minutes. Remove from pan to paper towels to cool completely.

Pumpkin Seeds with Cinnamon and Salt

4 cups pumpkin seeds
Nonstick cooking spray
1 tsp. salt
½ tsp. ground cinnamon

Preheat oven to 350°F. Spray shallow baking pan with cooking spray. Spread seeds out in even layer in prepared pan. Spray seeds lightly with cooking spray; sprinkle with half of the salt and cinnamon. Bake 5 minutes. Remove from oven. Stir seeds. Spray seeds lightly with cooking spray; sprinkle with remaining salt and cinnamon. Continue baking for 20 additional minutes or until seeds are toasted, stirring occasionally.

Pumpkin-Peanut Butter Dip

1 cup firmly packed brown sugar
¾ cup peanut butter
1 tsp. vanilla
¾ cup canned pumpkin

Mix sugar and peanut butter in small bowl. Stir in vanilla. Add pumpkin; mix until well blended. Serve with sliced apples, if desired.

Apple Dippers

4 oz. (½ of an 8-oz. package) cream cheese
¼ cup peanut butter
1 Tbs. mini chocolate chips
2 large apples, cut in slices

Mix cream cheese, peanut butter, and chocolate chips. Serve with apple slices for dipping.

Easy Fruit Dip

2 pkg. (8 oz. each) cream cheese, softened
1 jar (7 oz.) marshmallow creme
¼ cup milk
1½ tsp. vanilla
½ tsp. ground nutmeg
Assorted cut-up fruit

Beat cream cheese, marshmallow creme, milk, vanilla, and nutmeg with electric mixer until mixture is well blended and smooth. Spoon dip into serving bowl. Serve with fruit.

Fun Apple Dip

1 pkg. (8 oz.) cream cheese, softened
1 cup firmly packed brown sugar
1 tsp. vanilla
Pecan pieces (optional)

Mix cream cheese, sugar, and vanilla in medium bowl until smooth. Stir in nuts. Serve with apple slices, if desired.

Pumpkin Dip

4 oz. (½ of an 8-oz. package) cream cheese, softened
½ cup powdered sugar
3 Tbs. pumpkin pie spice
6 miniature pumpkins
Thin ginger cookies (such as Anna's Ginger Thins®)
Thin almond-cinnamon cookies (such as Anna's Almond Cinnamon Thins®)

Mix cream cheese, sugar, and pumpkin pie spice until well blended. Slice off top of each pumpkin, including stem, to create "lid." Remove pulp from inside the pumpkin. Insert small cup or bowl inside pumpkin cavity. Fill cup with pumpkin dip, cover with pumpkin "lid." Serve with cookies. Makes 6 servings.

Harvest "Thyme" Roasted Sweet Potato Wedges

3 Tbs. brown sugar
2 Tbs. olive oil
1 tsp. kosher salt
½ tsp. ground pepper
¼ tsp. ground nutmeg
4 lbs. small sweet potatoes, peeled, each cut into 8 wedges
8 sprigs fresh thyme, chopped

Preheat oven to 400°F. Mix sugar, oil, salt, pepper, and nutmeg in large bowl. Add potatoes; toss to coat. Arrange potatoes in single layer in large shallow baking pan. Sprinkle with thyme. Bake potatoes 1 hour or until the edges are dark brown and wedges are crisp, turning after 30 minutes.

Pumpkin Butter Spread

1 jar (9 oz.) Eckert's® Pumpkin Butter
1 pkg. (8 oz.) cream cheese, softened

Mix pumpkin butter and cream cheese together until well blended. Serve with sliced crisp Eckert's® apples, slices of fresh baked bread, bagels, or crackers.

Apple and Brie Soup

3 Tbs. unsalted butter

2 large apples (about 1 lb.), peeled, cored, and cut into 1-inch cubes

1 sweet yellow onion, peeled, chopped

1 stalk celery, chopped

2½ cups of chicken stock or water

2 Tbs. flour

½ tsp. white pepper

1 tsp. ground ginger

1 tsp. ground cumin

8 oz. Brie cheese, rind trimmed, cut into cubes

Salt, to taste

¼ cup heavy cream

Melt butter in Dutch oven or large saucepan over medium heat. Add apples, onions, and celery; cook and stir 8 to 10 minutes or until vegetables are soft. Stir in flour; cook 2 minutes, stirring constantly. Gradually add stock while constantly stirring apple mixture with whisk. Stir in pepper, ginger, and cumin. Bring to boil. Reduce heat to medium-low; simmer 15 minutes. Remove from heat. Purée soup, in batches, in blender or food processor until smooth; return puréed mixture to same pan. Cook on medium heat until heated through. Add cheese; stir until cheese is melted and mixture is well blended. Add salt to taste. Stir in cream with whisk just before serving. Serve with good bread, if desired.

From Our Farm

Apples need to be cross-pollinated (meaning two different varieties of apples need to be grown near each other). Consequently, during apple bloom, we rent millions of bees, from an apiarist, to help transfer pollen among the trees. Without cross-pollination, our apple crop would be very small.

Butternut Squash and Pear Soup

4 Tbs. unsalted butter

2 large onions, diced

1 medium butternut squash, peeled, seeded, and cut into 1-inch pieces

4 medium Bosc, Anjou, or Comice pears, peeled; 3 chopped into 1-inch pieces and 1 finely diced for garnish

1 quart reduced-sodium chicken or vegetable stock

2 rosemary sprigs

½ cup heavy cream

Salt

Freshly ground black pepper

Sugar

Heat butter in large pot over medium heat until melted and bubbling. Add onions and cook until softened and starting to turn translucent. Add squash and pears and cook 5 minutes. Add stock. Ingredients should be submerged in liquid. If not, add just enough water to do so. Add rosemary, bring to a simmer, and cook until squash and pears are very tender, about 45 minutes. Remove rosemary sprigs. Purée in pot with a stick blender until smooth. Or, do in batches in the blender. Add in heavy cream and mix by hand. Season with salt, pepper, and sugar to taste. Place heap of diced pear in the middle of each serving bowl, then surround with soup. Serves 8-10.

Beet and Apple Soup

6 beets, trimmed and quartered 1 onion, quartered 1 clove garlic 4 cups unsweetened apple juice 3 Tbs. fresh lemon juice 1 Tbs. sour cream Salt and pepper	Place beets, onion, garlic, and apple juice in large saucepan. Bring to boil on medium-high heat. Reduce heat to medium-low; simmer 25 minutes. Purée beet mixture, in batches, in blender. Stir in lemon juice. Season to taste with salt and pepper. Top each serving with a swirl of sour cream.

Apple Slaw

2 cups shredded cabbage 1½ cups red apples, finely chopped ⅓ cup raisins ½ cup coleslaw dressing	Combine cabbage, apples, raisins, and dressing. Refrigerate until ready to serve. Makes 4 servings.

—— *From Our Kitchen* ——

For a basic cole slaw dressing, mix ½ cup plain yogurt with 2 Tbs. each Dijon and mayo, plus 2 tsp. sugar. Salt and pepper to taste.

Spinach and Apple Salad with Vinaigrette

VINAIGRETTE

¼ cup vegetable oil

3 Tbs. apple cider vinegar

½ tsp. honey Dijon mustard

¾ tsp. caraway seeds

½ tsp. dried tarragon, crumbled

½ tsp. granulated sugar

Dash white pepper

SALAD

1 large bunch fresh spinach, washed, torn into bite-sized pieces (about 6 cups)

6 slices bacon, crisply cooked, drained, and crumbled

3 green onions, diagonally sliced

2 Granny Smith apples, chopped

¾ cup crumbled blue cheese or shredded cheddar

TO PREPARE VINAIGRETTE: Mix oil, vinegar, mustard, caraway, tarragon, sugar, and pepper until well blended; set aside.

TO PREPARE SALAD: Toss together spinach, bacon, and onions in large bowl. Top with chopped apples and cheese. Drizzle with vinaigrette; toss lightly. Makes 4 to 6 servings.

—— *From Our Family Album* ——

Grandma Eckert always kept a quart mason jar of her vinaigrette dressing, stored and ready, in the refrigerator.

Warm Spinach Salad with Apples, Bacon, and Cranberries

1 pkg. (10 oz.) fresh baby spinach
1 small Eckert's® apple, sliced (about 1 cup)
¾ cup thinly sliced red onions
½ cup dried cranberries, chopped
⅓ cup reduced balsamic vinegar or 2 Tbs. balsamic glaze
2 Tbs. cranberry juice
1 Tbs. sugar
1 tsp. Dijon-style mustard
¼ tsp. salt
¼ tsp. freshly ground black pepper
3 Tbs. sour cream
4 slices bacon, cooked, drained, and crumbled

Toss together spinach, apple, onions, and cranberries in large salad bowl. Combine vinegar, cranberry juice, sugar, mustard, salt, and pepper in small saucepan. Bring to boil over medium heat; continue to boil for 1 minute, stirring occasionally. Remove from heat. Allow to cool 5 to 6 minutes. Stir in sour cream. Drizzle dressing over spinach mixture; toss to coat. Sprinkle with bacon. Serve immediately. Makes about 6 (2-cup) servings.

Fuji Apple-Spinach Salad

DRESSING
6 Tbs. apple cider vinegar
¼ cup red onion, finely chopped
3 Tbs. sugar
1 clove garlic, minced (optional)
¼ tsp. salt
⅛ tsp. freshly ground black pepper
½ cup olive oil

SALAD
½ cup slivered almonds
2 Tbs. sugar
1 pkg. (6 oz.) baby spinach leaves
1 head Romaine lettuce, torn into bite-sized pieces
2 Fuji apples, cored, thinly sliced

TO PREPARE DRESSING: Mix vinegar, onion, sugar, garlic, salt, and pepper in small bowl with wire whisk until well blended. Gradually add oil, stirring constantly with whisk.

TO PREPARE SALAD: Place nuts and sugar in medium skillet. Cook over medium-high heat 4 minutes or until nuts are well-coated with sugar and browned, stirring constantly; set aside. Toss together spinach, lettuce, and apples in large bowl. Pour dressing over salad just before serving; toss. Sprinkle with almonds.

Cran-Apple Soufflé

1 pkg. (3 oz.) strawberry gelatin
1 cup boiling water
½ cup mayonnaise
1 Tbs. fresh lemon juice
¼ tsp. salt
½ tsp. cinnamon
2 apples
1 cup whole cranberries or 1 can (8 oz.) cranberry sauce
¼ cup nuts, chopped
¾ cup miniature marshmallows

In a mixing bowl, dissolve gelatin in boiling water. Stir in mayonnaise and beat until very smooth; add lemon juice, salt, and cinnamon. Chill until slightly firm, then beat until fluffy. Pare and dice apples. Fold in apples, cranberries, nuts, and marshmallows. Pour into a 1-quart mold. Chill until very firm. When ready to serve, run warm water on the outside surface of mold and invert onto a serving dish. Garnish with additional cranberries. Serves 4.

Apple Cider Vinaigrette

¼ cup cider vinegar
2 tsp. Dijon-style mustard
Salt and freshly ground black pepper, to taste
¼ cup olive oil

Mix vinegar, mustard, salt, and pepper in small bowl with wire whisk until well blended. Gradually add oil, stirring constantly with whisk. Continue mixing until vinaigrette is slightly thickened.

Tossed Greens with Pineapple, Apple, and Feta Cheese

3 Tbs. balsamic vinegar
4 Tbs. vegetable oil
3 Tbs. water
2 Tbs. Eckert's® Hot & Sharp Mustard
1 clove garlic, minced
Salt and pepper, to taste
6 cups torn leaf lettuce leaves
1½ cups chopped pineapple (¾-inch cubes)
2 medium Red Delicious apples, cored and thinly sliced, unpeeled
3 Tbs. crumbled Feta cheese

Mix vinegar, oil, water, mustard, and garlic in small bowl with wire whisk until well blended. Season with salt and pepper. Toss together lettuce, pineapple, apples, and cheese in large bowl. Drizzle with vinaigrette; toss gently. Serve immediately.

Apple Delight Salad

2 heads leaf lettuce
2 Gala or Honeycrisp apples, cut in half, cored
2 tsp. fresh lemon juice
Salt and freshly ground black pepper, to taste
½ cup walnut halves
¼ cup + 1 Tbs. chopped fresh flat-leaf parsley
8 oz. blue cheese, cut into ½-inch chunks
Apple cider vinaigrette
(See page 12 for vinaigrette recipe)

Cut apples lengthwise into ¼-inch matchstick strips. Toss apple strips with lemon juice to prevent browning; set aside. Place leaf lettuce in large bowl; season with salt and pepper. Add walnuts, ¼ cup of parsley, and cheese. Drizzle with vinaigrette to taste; toss lightly. Divide evenly among 8 salad plates, if desired. Top with apple strips; sprinkle with remaining 1 tablespoon chopped parsley.

Eckert's® Waldorf Salad

2 cups red apples, finely chopped
1 cup celery, finely chopped
¼ cup pecans or walnuts, chopped
¾-1 cup mayonnaise
1 cup seedless grapes
Lettuce leaves
½ cup fresh or canned pineapple, chopped and drained (optional)

Combine apples, celery, and nuts in medium bowl; stir in enough mayonnaise to moisten. Add grapes or pineapple, if desired. Cover and refrigerate until ready to serve. Serve on lettuce leaves. Serves 5 to 6.

Apple, Cheese, Walnut Salad

VINAIGRETTE
3 Tbs. olive oil
2 Tbs. balsamic vinegar
2 tsp. Dijon-style mustard
1 clove garlic, crushed
Fresh ground black pepper, to taste

SALAD
8 cups torn mixed salad greens
2 medium Honeycrisp apples, halved, cored, and sliced ⅛-inch thick
⅓ cup crumbled blue cheese
¼ cup walnuts, toasted, coarsely chopped

TO PREPARE VINAIGRETTE: Mix oil, vinegar, mustard, and garlic in small bowl with wire whisk until well blended. Season with pepper.

TO PREPARE SALAD: Toss together greens and apple slices in large bowl. Drizzle with vinaigrette; toss lightly. Arrange salad on large serving platter; sprinkle with cheese and nuts.

Big Chop Apple Salad

DRESSING
½ cup vegetable oil
¼ cup rice vinegar
1 Tbs. balsamic vinegar
2 Tbs. sugar

SALAD
1 head Romaine lettuce
2 Fuji apples, chopped
1 red onion, chopped
¾ cup walnuts, chopped
6 oz. blue cheese crumbles
½ cup dried cranberries
4 slices of bacon, crisply cooked, drained, and crumbled

TO PREPARE DRESSING: Mix oil, vinegars, and sugar in small bowl with wire whisk until well blended.

TO PREPARE SALAD: Toss together lettuce, apples, and onions in large bowl. Top with nuts, cheese, cranberries, and bacon. Drizzle with dressing; toss lightly.

—— *From Our Farm* ——

Patience is a must for a fruit grower. We select fruit tree varieties three years before we plant them. We work with nurseries around the country to grow specific fruit varieties grafted on to dwarfing root stocks. After planting, it takes another three years until the trees bear a measurable volume of fruit in our orchards.

Eckert's® Crunchy Apple-Walnut Salad

¼ cup extra virgin olive oil
¼ cup apple juice
2 Tbs. balsamic vinegar
½ tsp. salt
¼ tsp. freshly ground black pepper
6 cups mixed salad greens
4 medium Honeycrisp (or other variety)
Apples, cored, cut into chunks
2 Tbs. toasted walnuts, chopped
3 Tbs. freshly grated Parmigiano-Reggiano

Add oil, juice, vinegar, salt, and pepper to small glass jar. Cover with tight-fitting lid; shake until mixture is well blended. Toss together greens, apples, and nuts in large bowl. Drizzle with dressing; toss lightly. Sprinkle with cheese.

Green Salad with Apple Cider Dressing

DRESSING
1 cup apple cider
2 Tbs. canola oil
1 Tbs. apple cider vinegar
1 tsp. Dijon-style mustard
½ tsp. molasses or pure maple syrup
Salt, to taste

TO PREPARE DRESSING: Bring cider to a simmer in small saucepan over medium heat. Continue simmering until cider is thick and reduced to about 2 tablespoons, stirring constantly. Remove from heat. Mix reduced cider, oil, vinegar, mustard, molasses, and salt until well blended.

SALAD
1 head red leaf lettuce
2 tart apples, chopped or thinly sliced
1 red onion, chopped
¾ cup candied nuts
6 oz. crumbled blue or Feta cheese
4 slices bacon, crisply cooked, drained, and crumbled

TO PREPARE SALAD: Toss together lettuce, apples, and onions in large bowl. Sprinkle with nuts, cheese, and bacon. Drizzle with dressing; toss lightly.

Baked Pear and Goat Cheese Salad

1½ Tbs. walnuts, finely chopped

3 Tbs. goat cheese, softened

2 pears, peeled, halved, and cored

Nonstick cooking spray

¼ cup raspberry vinegar

¼ cup honey

¼ tsp. ground ginger

¼ tsp. ground cinnamon

¼ tsp. salt

⅛ tsp. crushed red pepper flakes

6 cups mixed salad greens

Preheat oven to 400°F. Toast walnuts in small skillet over medium-high heat 1 to 2 minutes or until walnuts begin to brown, stirring constantly. Remove from heat. Mix goat cheese and walnuts. Place pear halves, cut-sides up, on ungreased shallow baking sheet. Spoon goat cheese mixture evenly into center of each pear. Lightly spray pears with cooking spray. Bake 20 minutes or until pears are just tender. Meanwhile, mix vinegar, honey, ginger, cinnamon, salt, and red pepper flakes with wire whisk until well blended. Toss greens with vinaigrette in large bowl. To serve, spoon 1½ cups greens mixture onto individual serving plate. Top with 1 pear half. Serves 4.

── *From Our Kitchen* ──

To deactivate the enzymes that turn the flesh of apples brown, make a solution including acidic ingredients. Dip apples in a bowl of ½ teaspoon ascorbic acid (vitamin C) to 2½ cups of water. (Products containing ascorbic acid can be found near canning supplies.) Or, use a pastry brush to apply a solution of 1 part lemon juice to 3 parts water. Alternatively, store sliced apples in a zip top bag filled with white soda. Drain and blot dry before using or serving.

Salad with Roasted Sweet Potatoes

SWEET POTATOES

2 sweet potatoes, peeled, cut into thin matchlike sticks

1 Tbs. olive oil

Coarsely ground salt and black pepper, to taste

SALAD

½ cup walnuts

2½ Tbs. olive oil

¼ tsp. ground red pepper (cayenne)

2 Tbs. lemon juice

1 tsp. honey

Coarsely ground salt and black pepper

4 oz. Feta cheese, crumbled

6 cups torn Romaine lettuce

TO PREPARE SWEET POTATOES: Arrange 2 oven racks about 6 inches apart in center of oven; preheat to 450°F. Grease shallow baking pan. Place sweet potatoes in single layer on pan. Drizzle with 1 tablespoon oil; toss to coat. Season with salt and black pepper. Bake on upper oven rack 20 to 30 minutes or until tender, stirring after 10 minutes.

TO PREPARE SALAD: Toss nuts with ½ teaspoon oil and red pepper. Bake on lower rack 3 minutes or until golden brown and lightly toasted. Mix lemon juice, honey, and remaining 2 tablespoons olive oil in large bowl; season with salt and black pepper. Add lettuce; toss lightly. Serve lettuce mixture topped with sweet potatoes, nuts, and cheese.

SAUCES & SIDE DISHES

Slow Cooker Sweet Vanilla Apples

3 lbs. firm cooking apples (such as Eckert's® Golden Delicious), peeled, sliced (7 to 8 large apples; about 9 cups)

¼ cup vanilla-flavored granulated sugar (See Tip)

¼-½ tsp. ground cinnamon

1 tsp. vanilla

Place apples and sugar in 3-quart slow cooker; toss to coat. Add cinnamon to taste; stir. Cover with lid. Cook on high for 30 minutes. Reduce to low. Cook apples until soft and tender, about 2 hours. (Do not overcook or apples will become mushy.) Stir in vanilla. Makes about 8 servings, ½ cup each. Serve hot over Eckert's® Frozen Custard with toasted pecans, if desired.

Chunky-Style Applesauce

8 large apples, peeled, thickly sliced

½ cup water or apple cider

½-¾ cup sugar

¼ tsp. ground cinnamon (optional)

Add apples and water to large saucepan; cover. Bring to boil on medium-high heat. Reduce heat to medium-low; simmer 10 minutes or until apples are tender. Mash apples with a potato masher to desired consistency; stir in sugar and cinnamon. Cook on low heat for 3 to 5 minutes or until heated through.

—— *From Our Kitchen* ——

Place two cups of granulated sugar in a sealable container (preferably glass). Cut a vanilla bean in half lengthwise and bury in the sugar. Cover tightly for at least 1 week to infuse flavor. Vanilla bean pieces may stay in the sugar indefinitely.

Vanilla sugar is excellent on fresh berries, oatmeal, and French toast. Use the dried vanilla bean pieces in hot milk for custards or puddings.

No-Cook Applesauce

1 small apple, peeled, cored
1 squeeze lemon juice
1½ tsp. sugar
Dash of ground cinnamon

Put apple and lemon juice in food processor. Process until very smooth. Stir in sugar to taste. Add cinnamon; mix well.

Easy Lodi Applesauce

8 large Lodi apples, peeled, thickly sliced
½ cup water
½-¾ cup sugar
¼ tsp. ground cinnamon

Add apples and water to large saucepan; cover. Bring to boil on medium-high heat. Reduce heat to medium-low; simmer 10 minutes or until apples are tender. Mash apples with potato masher to desired consistency; stir in sugar and cinnamon. Cook on low heat for 3 to 5 minutes or until heated through.

Butternut Squash, Apple, and Onion Pie

1 (9-inch) Eckert's® Pie Crust, thawed

2 Jonathan apples, cored, cut in half

½ of a butternut squash, seeded, cut in half, and peeled

1 small yellow onion

3 Tbs. unsalted butter, melted

2 tsp. chopped fresh rosemary

2 tsp. chopped fresh thyme

Kosher salt and black pepper

2 Tbs. whole-grain mustard

⅓ cup crumbled blue cheese

Preheat oven to 400°F. Cut apples, squash, and onion into ½-inch-thick slices; place in medium bowl. Add butter, rosemary, thyme, and salt and pepper to taste; toss to coat. Brush pie crust with mustard; fill crust with apple mixture. Cover edges of pie crust with pie crust shields or foil. Bake 45 minutes. Remove pie crust shields; bake an additional 10 minutes. Remove pie from oven; sprinkle with cheese. Bake an additional 5 minutes. Cool slightly before serving.

Apple and Sweet Potato Casserole

4 sweet potatoes, peeled, cut in
½-inch slices
2 large apples, peeled, sliced
⅛ tsp. salt
⅔ cup light corn syrup
⅔ cup firmly packed brown sugar
2 Tbs. butter
½ cup chopped pecans

Preheat oven to 350°F. Place potatoes in medium saucepan; add enough water to pan to completely cover potatoes. Stir in salt; bring to boil over medium-high heat. Continue boiling 10 minutes or until potatoes are just tender; drain. Place sweet potatoes in bottom of ungreased 13 × 9-inch baking pan; top with apples. Drizzle apples with corn syrup; sprinkle with brown sugar. Dot with butter; top with pecans. Cover pan with foil. Bake 35 minutes.

Grandma Ella's Apple-Cranberry Relish

1 seedless orange
12 oz. fresh cranberries
2 apples, peeled, cored
1 cup sugar

Cut orange in quarters, leaving peel intact; place in food processor. Add cranberries and apples; process until fruit is finely chopped. Stir in sugar. Refrigerate until ready to serve.

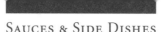
Stewed Apples

½ cup sugar

⅓ cup candy cinnamon imperial (such as Red Hots®)

4 to 5 cooking apples, peeled, quartered

Place sugar and candies in a large saucepan. Add just enough water to cover; stir. Bring to a boil over medium-high heat. Remove from heat; add apples and enough additional water to cover apples. Cook on medium heat until apples are tender.

Fried Apples

3 large cooking apples, cored

2 Tbs. brown sugar

3 Tbs. butter or margarine

Cut apples into ½- to ¾-inch-thick rings; sprinkle with sugar. Melt butter in large skillet over medium heat. Add apples; cook until tender, turning occasionally.

Celery-Apple Stuffing

½ cup butter or margarine
¾ cup minced onion
1 cup celery, finely chopped
1 egg, lightly beaten
1 cup turkey or chicken broth
2 tsp. parsley flakes
1 tsp. salt
½ tsp. pepper
2 loaves stale bread, cubed
1 cup apples, finely chopped
½ cup raisins (optional)

Preheat oven to 325°F. Melt butter in small skillet over low heat. Add onions and celery; cook and stir until onions are translucent. Mix egg, broth, parsley, salt, and pepper until well blended. Add bread cubes, apples, raisins, and onion mixture. Gradually add a small amount of water or milk if all bread is not moistened. Spoon into greased 2-quart baking dish. Bake 30 to 40 minutes or until heated through. For moister stuffing, cover dish with foil for first 10 minutes of baking time. Makes 8 servings.

Aunt Juanita's Stuffed Cinnamon Apples

½ cup sugar
½ cup water
½ cup candy cinnamon imperial (such as Red Hots®)
6 whole cloves
6 large baking apples
1 cup cottage cheese
4 Tbs. chopped nuts
⅓ cup mayonnaise
Lettuce

Combine sugar, water, candy, and cloves in large saucepan. Bring to boil on medium-high heat. Continue cooking until candies are dissolved and syrup is red, stirring occasionally. Remove from heat. Peel apples, leaving them whole; cut a 1-inch-diameter hole in the center of each apple to remove core. Add apples to syrup mixture in saucepan. Return syrup to boil; cook apples until tender and red, turning frequently. Remove apples from syrup; drain. Discard liquid. Refrigerate apples 1 hour or until chilled. Combine cottage cheese and nuts; stir in mayonnaise. Spoon evenly into center of apples. Serve stuffed apples on bed of lettuce.

—— *From Our Family Album* ——

Aunt Juanita always brought cinnamon apples to our Thanksgiving and Christmas family gatherings. The bright red apples look beautiful on the dinner table.

Eckert's

Always in Season

Eckert's Apple Varieties

For over 100 years Eckert's has been growing traditional apple favorites, as well as introducing new and unique varieties.

Selecting apples is the same regardless of variety. Look for apples that are free of bruises. Choose apples that are fragrant, and are firm to the touch.

Here are some of Eckert's favorite homegrown apple varieties. Each are unique in flavor and texture, thus differing in their best overall uses.

HONEYCRISP *Ripens Late August*

This apple is a cross between a Macoun and Honeygold and ripens towards the end of August, or the beginning of September. It is highly popular for its crispness and is a great apple for fresh eating.

JONATHAN *Ripens Early September*

Jonathans are the first red apple of fall, ripening in early September. It has a sweet-tart flavor with a firm texture and is used mostly for fresh eating and cooking.

JONAGOLD *Ripens in September*

A brilliant cross between Jonathan and Golden Delicious, it inherits a sweet and tangy flavor and excellent fresh eating and cooking qualities.

GOLDEN DELICIOUS *Ripens Mid-September*

This all-purpose apple is known for its firm white flesh and rich mild flavor when baked or cooked. The tender skin overwrapping a mellow, sweet flavor makes this an appealing choice for fresh eating.

RED DELICIOUS *Ripens Mid-September*

An American classic! Red Delicious has been a favorite for decades. Its beautiful shiny color and broad shape makes it an excellent addition to fresh salads and gift baskets.

FUJI *Ripens Early October*

America's new favorite! This super sweet and crispy apple originated from Japan, but America has now become its leading producer of this apple. Fujis ripen in October and are great for topping salads and fresh eating.

GRANNY SMITH *Ripens October*

This large apple with its beautiful green color is best known for its sour and tart flavor. Ripening in October, its tart flavor contrasts well with sweet caramel and covered with your favorite topping.

Eckert's® Old-Fashioned Outdoor Apple Butter

1 barrel of apple cider

7–8 bushels of pared, cored, and quartered apples

20 lbs. sugar

4 Tbs. cinnamon

1 Tbs. ground cloves

This recipe is for cooking large amounts of apple butter over an outdoor open fire. It was used at harvest time by the Eckert families. They would cook down one barrel of apple cider to half a barrel on one day. On the next day, they would add 7–8 bushels of pared, cored, and quartered apples, 20 pounds sugar, 4 tablespoons cinnamon, and 1 tablespoon ground cloves. They stirred the butter constantly until it began to thicken and cooked it for 6–8 hours. It was then cooled and taken to the market for sale. What's next? Grandma Eckert would say, "You get up and do it all over again the next day!"

APPLE SELECTION & STORAGE

Apples should be stored by themselves, since they naturally emit ethylene gas, which can cause other fruits and vegetables to quickly turn soft and spoil. Apples soften quickly, 6–10 times faster at room temperature than if refrigerated. Cooler temperatures help maintain quality, nutrition, juiciness, and crispness.

Eckert's®
Kitchen Apple Butter

1 gal. Eckert's® Apple Cider

5 lbs. apples, peeled, cored

2 lbs. sugar

1 to 2 tsp. allspice (optional)

2 to 3 tsp. cinnamon (optional)

1 to 2 tsp. cloves (optional)

Bring apple cider to boil in large stockpot; continue cooking until cider is reduced ⅔ to ½ of the original amount. Reduce heat to low; add apples. Cook until consistency of apples becomes like that of a fruit butter and color darkens, stirring constantly to prevent scorching. Stir in sugar, allspice, cinnamon, and cloves. Makes 6 pints.

APPLE NUTRITION

One medium-sized fresh apple with the skin has about 80 calories, 5 grams of fiber, and 20 grams of carbohydrates. It is a good idea to eat apples with their skin. Almost half of the vitamin C content is found just underneath the skin and two-thirds of the fiber is found in the skin.

ESTIMATED APPLE YIELD

1 lb. of apples = about 3 medium apples

1 lb. of apples = about 2 cups sliced

2 lbs. of apples = one 9-inch pie

1 bushel of apples = 48 lbs.

1 bushel of apples = about 126 medium apples

1 bushel of apples = 16–20 qts. sliced & canned

1 bushel of apples = 20–24 qts. applesauce

About 36 apples will make 1 gal. apple cider

Basic Squash Preparation

1. Wash squash under cool running water until all the dirt has been removed.

2. Using a cleaver or large knife, cut the squash in half (lengthwise or crosswise) and remove the seeds and stringy fibers from the cavity with a spoon. Winter squash can be difficult to cut, and it is sometimes easier to bake the squash first for 25 or 30 minutes or microwave on high for 5 or 10 minutes and then let it stand for a few minutes before trying to cut it in half.

3. Once the squash is cut in half and seeds removed, it can be quartered, cubed, or sliced if required. Otherwise, cook squash as directed.

If the squash is going to be cooked whole, be sure to pierce the skin in several places to allow steam to escape and prevent squash from exploding.

Roast: 350°F, cut-side down, pierce skin several times, bake for 50–120 minutes

Boil: not recommended because squash becomes too watery

Microwave: in plastic 15–20 minutes

Recommended to serve with 1 tablespoon butter & ½ tablespoon brown sugar

carnival squash

butternut squash

acorn squash

spaghetti squash

Toasted Pumpkin (or Squash) Seeds

To Clean: Separate the pumpkin seeds from the stringy membrane of a freshly carved pumpkin. Rinse the pumpkin seeds in a colander, until they are free of any membrane matter. Dry with paper towels.

To Roast or Toast: Coat ½ cup of seeds with 1 teaspoon olive oil and ½ teaspoon seasoning of your choice. **NOTE:** You can use any seasoning blend you like. Adjust the amount to your taste buds.

Place in 250°F oven for about 1 hour, stirring every 15 minutes. They are done when they are light brown in color.

Additional Seasoning Ideas: Try additional seasonings on your pumpkin seeds: Cajun seasoning, Worcestershire sauce, soy sauce, and garlic salt are some of the many possibilities.

Storing: Store baked pumpkin seeds in an airtight container.

Spaghetti Squash Bake

1 spaghetti squash
4 oz. shredded mozzarella
1 jar spaghetti sauce
2 tsp. dry basil

Preheat oven to 350°F. Slice squash in half and place flesh-side down in a baking dish. Add ¼ inch of water. Bake for 40 minutes, or until tender and remove. Rake squash with a fork, creating "spaghetti" strands. Spoon on sauce, mozzarella, and basil. Place back in oven and bake until cheese begins to bubble. Serve warm.

Standard Double-Crust Pie Shell

3 cups all-purpose flour

1½ tsp. salt

1 cup + 2 Tbs. lard or
solid vegetable shortening

7-8 Tbs. ice water

In large bowl, combine flour and salt. With a pastry blender, 2 forks, or fingers, blend in lard or shortening until mixture particles are the size of peas. Sprinkle in a tablespoon of water at a time until the mixture forms a ball. Divide dough in half and wrap in plastic. Refrigerate for at least 20 minutes to facilitate easier rolling. Roll out each ball separately on a floured surface into a circular shape about ⅛-inch thick. Use only enough flour to prevent sticking. Transfer dough to pie pan. Press dough together if it breaks when transferred. Makes two 10-inch pie crusts. Trim to fit smaller pie pans.

WHAT TO DO WITH PIE CRUST TRIMMINGS:

If you have trimmings, sprinkle the extra dough with cinnamon and sugar. Bake them on a sheet pan until they just begin to brown. Snack on these while your pie bakes!

WHY USE LARD IN PIE CRUSTS?

Experienced bakers in our family believe lard makes the flakiest and best-tasting crust. Leaf lard is the highest grade of lard. Although it is a little trickier to come by, it has the mildest flavor and the longest shelf-life. Check with your local butcher shop for leaf lard.

Pumpkin Succotash

1 pie pumpkin
1 cup chicken or vegetable broth or water
2 Tbs. butter or olive oil
2 large onions, peeled and sliced
1 pkg. (10 oz.) frozen corn
Salt and black pepper, to taste
Dash of ground red pepper (cayenne) (optional)

Peel pumpkin; cut enough of the pulp into 2-inch cubes to make 4 cups. Place pumpkin pulp in Dutch oven or large saucepan. Stir in broth, butter, and onions; cover. Bring to boil on medium-high heat. Reduce heat to low; simmer 15 minutes or until pulp is tender. Stir in corn, salt, and black and red pepper. Continue cooking 5 to 8 minutes or until corn is heated through. Makes 6 to 8 servings.

Sassy Apple Slaw with Walnuts

⅔ cup mayonnaise
¼ cup white wine vinegar
¼ cup apple cider
½ tsp. salt
¼ tsp. freshly ground pepper
½ head of cabbage, cored, coarsely shredded
1 Granny Smith apple, peeled, coarsely grated
¾ cup walnuts, chopped, toasted
¼ cup parsley, finely chopped

Mix mayonnaise, vinegar, cider, salt, and pepper until well blended. Toss together cabbage and apple in large bowl. Add mayonnaise mixture, nuts, and parsley; toss until blended. Cover and refrigerate 1 hour before serving.

Brown Rice with Apples and Golden Raisins

1½ cups chicken broth	Add broth, water, rice, and salt to medium
1 cup water	saucepan; bring to boil over high heat. Cover;
1 cup brown rice	reduce heat to medium-low. Cook 45 to 55
¼ tsp. coarse salt	minutes or until rice is tender and all liquid
2 Tbs. olive oil	has been absorbed. Heat oil in large skillet over
1 apple, cored, chopped	medium heat, swirling oil to coat bottom of pan.
1 large shallot, peeled, minced	Add apples, shallots, celery, raisins, and nuts.
1 stalk of celery, finely chopped	Cook and stir 5 minutes or until celery is tender.
⅓ cup golden raisins	Add rice mixture to skillet; stir. Makes 6 servings.
⅓ cup walnuts, chopped	

Sweet Potatoes in Orange Cups

4 oranges	Preheat oven to 350°F. Cut oranges in half
2 cups mashed sweet potatoes	crosswise. Scrape out membranes using melon
¼ cup pecans, chopped	baller or teaspoon. Carefully remove pulp; reserve
1 tsp. grated orange zest	pulp for another use. Combine sweet potatoes,
¾ tsp. ground cinnamon	pecans, zest, and cinnamon. Fill each orange cup
	with ¼ cup of the potato mixture. Place orange
	cups in large muffin pan; cover with foil. Bake 20
	minutes or until heated through. Top each with
	curled orange peel, if desired.

Brandied Sweet Potatoes

2 lbs. sweet potatoes, peeled
½ cup firmly packed brown sugar
3 Tbs. butter or margarine
3 Tbs. brandy or water
½ tsp. salt

Place potatoes in Dutch oven or large saucepan; add enough water to pan to cover potatoes completely. Bring to boil over medium-high heat. Continue cooking 30 to 35 minutes or until potatoes are tender; drain. Cool slightly; cut crosswise into ½-inch-thick slices. Cook sugar, butter, brandy, and salt in large skillet over medium heat until bubbly, stirring constantly. Add potato slices; cook until potatoes are glazed with the sugar mixture, turning occasionally. Makes 6 to 8 servings.

Fried Sweet Potatoes

½ cup sugar
2 tsp. ground cinnamon
8 cups vegetable oil
5 lbs. sweet potatoes, peeled, cut crosswise into ½-inch slices

Mix sugar and cinnamon. Heat oil in electric fryer or large saucepan to 360°F. Fry sweet potatoes, in batches, 8 minutes or until golden brown. Drain on paper towels. Sprinkle immediately with cinnamon sugar.

Orange-Honey Acorn Squash

3 small acorn squash	Preheat oven to 400°F. Cut each squash in half; remove and discard seeds. Place squash, cut-sides up, in shallow baking pan. Mix juice concentrate and honey. Dot each squash half with ½ teaspoon butter. Cover tightly with foil; bake 30 minutes. Remove foil; bake an additional 30 minutes or until squash is tender. Scoop out squash flesh; mash with potato masher. Stir in juice concentrate mixture; spoon squash mixture back into shells. Bake 10 minutes. Makes 6 servings.
¼ cup frozen orange juice concentrate, thawed	
2 Tbs. honey	
1 Tbs. butter	
¼ tsp. ground nutmeg or ground cinnamon	

Squash with Herbs

2 lbs. butternut or buttercup squash	Cut each squash in half lengthwise; remove and discard seeds. Add ¼ inch of water to 13 × 9-inch baking dish; place squash, cut-sides down, in dish. Bake 45 minutes or until squash is tender; drain. Cut into serving-size pieces; return to dish, shell-side down. Preheat broiler. Brush squash with oil; sprinkle with basil, thyme, and rosemary. Top with cheese. Broil, 4 inches from heat, until cheese is melted and golden.
2 Tbs. olive oil	
2 Tbs. chopped fresh basil	
1½ tsp. chopped fresh thyme	
1 tsp. chopped fresh rosemary or ¼ tsp. dry rosemary leaves, crushed	
1 cup shredded mozzarella cheese	

Acorn Squash Rings

2 large acorn squash (about 1½ lbs. each)
¼ cup butter
2 Tbs. maple syrup
1 large Golden Delicious apple; cut into ½-inch pieces
1 large Red Delicious apple, cut into ½-inch pieces
1 banana, sliced
1 orange, sectioned, cut into 1-inch pieces
½-1 tsp. curry powder, to taste
¼-1 tsp. pepper, to taste
¼ tsp. salt
2 Tbs. toasted chopped almonds

Preheat oven to 350°F. Line 15 × 10 × 1-inch shallow baking pan with foil. Cut squash crosswise into 1-inch-thick slices; arrange in single layer in prepared pan. Bring butter and syrup to a boil in medium saucepan on medium-high heat; remove from heat. Brush syrup mixture onto squash rings. Cover with foil; bake 30 minutes. Add apples to remaining syrup mixture in saucepan; cook on medium heat 3 minutes or until crisp-tender. Stir in banana, orange, curry powder, pepper, and salt; cook until heated through. Arrange squash rings on serving dish. Fill centers with apple mixture; sprinkle with nuts. Makes 8 servings.

Apple and Winter Squash

2 winter squash (such as acorn or butternut)
2 Tbs. unsalted butter
½ cup onions, finely chopped
1 cup apples, chopped
2 Tbs. brown sugar
1 Tbs. balsamic vinegar
½ tsp. dried thyme leaves
¼ tsp. salt

Preheat oven to 375°F. Cut each squash lengthwise in half; remove and discard seeds. Arrange squash, cut-sides up, in 13 × 9-inch baking dish. Melt butter in a large skillet over medium heat. Add onions; cook and stir 3 minutes. Add apples, brown sugar, balsamic vinegar, thyme, and salt; cook and stir an additional 3 minutes. Remove from heat; set aside. Score squash by making shallow cuts across the surface; spoon apple mixture evenly into squash. Add ½ inch of water to same 13 × 9-inch baking dish; add squash. Cover with foil. Bake 1 hour or until squash is tender. Makes 4 to 6 servings.

Butternut Squash Fries with Maple Cream

1 butternut squash, halved lengthwise, seeded and peeled

2 tsp. extra virgin olive oil

½ cup sour cream

2 Tbs. maple syrup

3 Tbs. ground cumin

1 tsp. salt

½ tsp. chili powder

2 limes, cut into wedges

Preheat oven to 425°F. Cut squash into ½-inch-wide, 3-inch-long sticks; place in large bowl. Add oil; toss to coat. Spread squash in single layer on foil-lined baking sheet. Cook 35 minutes or until fries are tender when pierced with a knife and golden. Meanwhile, mix sour cream and syrup; set aside. Combine cumin, salt, and chili powder; sprinkle over fries. Serve with maple cream, remaining seasoned salt, and lime wedges.

Maple-Squash Purée

5 lbs. butternut squash, peeled, seeded, and cut into 1-inch pieces (about 10 cups)

2 cups water

1¾ tsp. salt, divided

⅓ cup maple syrup

3 Tbs. unsalted butter

½ tsp. black pepper

Place water, 1 teaspoon of salt, and squash in large saucepan; cover. Bring to a boil over medium-high heat; reduce heat to medium-low. Simmer 15 minutes or until squash is very tender. Drain squash, reserving ½ cup of the cooking liquid. Purée squash, maple syrup, and butter, in batches, in food processor until smooth, adding some of the reserved cooking liquid if purée is too thick. Transfer to serving bowl; stir in pepper and remaining ¾ teaspoon salt.

—— *From Our Kitchen* ——

Purée can be made up to 3 days ahead and stored in refrigerator. Reheat in microwave, double boiler, or preheated 350°F oven, adding water as needed, before serving. Maple-Squash Purée with Bacon and Ginger: Stir in 6 bacon slices, crumbled, and 1 teaspoon finely grated fresh gingerroot along with the pepper.

Zucchini Casserole

2 Tbs. butter, plus extra butter for greasing casserole dish

2 Tbs. finely chopped onions, about ¼ of a small onion

1 garlic clove, minced

8 oz. fresh mushrooms, sliced

1 tsp. salt

½ tsp. dried oregano leaves

8 cups zucchini, unpeeled and thinly sliced (3 to 4 medium)

3 to 4 Tbs. fresh flat-leaf parsley, optional

1-1½ cups cheddar cheese, grated

½ cup seasoned dry bread crumbs

3 to 4 Tbs. Parmesan cheese, grated

Preheat oven to 325°F if using a glass 2-quart ovenproof casserole dish (350°F for a metal 2-quart pan). Butter the casserole dish; set aside. Melt butter in a 12-inch skillet on medium heat. Add onions and garlic; sauté about 1 to 2 minutes or until slightly soft. Stir in mushrooms and cook 5 to 6 minutes or until beginning to soften. Mix in salt and oregano leaves. Remove from heat.

In a 4-quart mixing bowl, combine mushroom mixture, zucchini, and parsley. Toss gently. Pour into prepared casserole. In a 1-quart bowl, mix cheddar cheese, dry bread crumbs, and Parmesan cheese. Sprinkle over top of zucchini.

Cover with aluminum foil and bake in preheated oven 30 minutes. Remove foil and continue to bake until vegetables are firm but tender, about 15 to 20 minutes. Topping will be lightly browned. Makes 4 to 5 servings.

Zucchini-Parmesan Supreme

1 zucchini, sliced ⅛-inch thick

1 large tomato, sliced

Salt and coarsely ground pepper, to taste

¼ cup chopped onions

3 cloves garlic, minced

1 cup freshly grated Parmesan cheese

½ tsp. dried thyme leaves

1 large tomato, chopped

½ cup seasoned dry bread crumbs

Preheat oven to 375°F. Layer ½ of the zucchini in bottom of 2-quart baking dish; cover with tomato slices. Season with salt and pepper; top with onions and garlic. Cover with remaining zucchini. Sprinkle with cheese, thyme, chopped tomatoes, and bread crumbs. Bake 30 minutes or until zucchini is soft. Makes 4 servings.

Wild Rice-Stuffed Squash

2 acorn squash, cut in half, seeded
½ cup wild rice, cooked
1 tsp. orange zest
½ cup walnuts, chopped
1 to 2 Tbs. thawed frozen orange juice concentrate

Preheat oven to 400°F. Combine rice, zest, nuts, and juice concentrate. Place squash in 13 × 9-inch baking pan; fill squash evenly with rice mixture. Cover with foil. Bake 35 minutes or until squash is tender. Drizzle additional thawed frozen orange juice concentrate over squash just before serving, if desired. Makes 4 servings.

Stuffed Squash

4 small acorn squash (1 to 1¼ lbs. each)
2 Tbs. unsalted butter, cut into 4 pieces
½ pound ground pork
1 Tbs. olive oil
¼ cup onions, chopped
1/4 cup celery, chopped
1/4 cup carrots, chopped
½ cup white wine
1½ cups cooked rice
1 box (9 oz.) frozen spinach, thawed, well drained
½ cup pine nuts, toasted
1½ tsp. dried oregano
Generous pinch kosher salt
Freshly ground black pepper

Preheat oven to 400°F. Line shallow baking pan with parchment paper. Slice 1 inch off top of each acorn squash; set aside for later use. Remove and discard seeds. Cut thin slice from rounded bottom of each squash. Place squash in pan, standing upright on sliced bottoms; fill evenly with butter. Set aside. Brown meat in large skillet over medium heat; drain. Remove meat from pan; cover to keep warm. Heat oil in same skillet. Add onions, celery, and carrots; cook and stir 7 to 10 minutes or until carrots are crisp-tender. Add wine, stirring to scrape up browned bits from bottom of skillet. Stir in meat, rice, spinach, nuts, and oregano. Season with salt and pepper to taste. Cook 2 to 3 minutes or until meat mixture is heated through, stirring constantly. Remove from heat. Spoon meat mixture evenly into squash; cover with tops. Bake 1 hour or until squash is tender.

Oven-Fried Sweet Potatoes

4 sweet potatoes (about 1½ lbs.),
peeled, cut into ¼-inch slices

1 Tbs. olive oil

¼ tsp. salt

¼ tsp. pepper

Nonstick cooking spray

1 Tbs. fresh parsley, finely chopped

1 tsp. orange zest

1 small garlic clove, minced

Preheat oven to 400°F. Combine potatoes, oil, salt, and pepper in large bowl; toss to coat. Arrange sweet potato slices in single layer on large baking sheet sprayed with cooking spray. Bake 30 minutes or until potatoes are tender, turning after 15 minutes. Mix parsley, orange zest, and garlic; sprinkle over potatoes.

Grammie's Sweet Potatoes

4 to 5 sweet potatoes

1 cup firmly packed brown sugar

½ cup margarine

Place sweet potatoes in large saucepan; add enough water to pan to completely cover potatoes. Bring to boil over medium-high heat; continue cooking 20 minutes or until potatoes are tender. Drain potatoes; cool slightly. Peel potatoes; cut into slices. Melt margarine in large skillet on medium heat. Stir in brown sugar; cook 1 minute, stirring occasionally. Add sweet potatoes, in batches. Cook until browned on both sides, turning once. Serve with additional margarine and sugar, if desired.

—— *From Our Family Album* ——

Grammie always made her special sweet potatoes for Thanksgiving dinner. (She used an electric skillet on medium.) They are always a hit with kids and adults!

Root Vegetable Fries

1 lb. parsnips, peeled

¾ lb. rutabagas, peeled

¾ lb. carrots (baby or peeled regular)

4 Tbs. extra virgin olive oil (approx.)

Sea salt and ground pepper, to taste

Preheat to 400°F. Cut parsnips, rutabagas, and regular carrots into long ½-inch-wide strips. Cut baby carrots in half if carrots are thick. Toss parsnips with 2 tablespoons of the oil in medium bowl; place parsnips in single layer on one end of large baking sheet. Toss rutabagas in same bowl with 1 tablespoon of oil; place in single layer on baking sheet. Repeat with carrots. Bake carrots about 40 minutes, parsnips about 50 minutes, and rutabagas about 1 hour or until each vegetable is golden brown, turning occasionally. Remove each vegetable from oven when it is done, then return any remaining vegetables to oven to finish cooking. Toss vegetables to combine; season with salt and pepper.

ENTRÉES

─── *From Our Family Album* ───

Eckert's first pick-your-own operation opened in Grafton, Illinois, in 1963, by Lary Eckert, pictured here on the tractor. The pick-your-own experience allowed customers a high volume of apples at an affordable price. Guests often walked away with 100-plus pounds of apples. Today, Eckert's three farms host more than 600,000 visitors.

Pork Chops with Apple Stuffing

2 Tbs. oil, divided
¼ cup onion, finely chopped
¼ cup celery, finely chopped
Few sprigs of parsley, chopped
2 cups dry bread crumbs
6 bone-in pork chops, 1-inch thick
Salt and pepper
Flour
3 tart apples, cut in half, cored

Preheat oven to 350°F. Melt 1 tablespoon of the oil in medium skillet over medium heat. Add onion, celery, and parsley; cook and stir until onion is translucent. Stir in bread crumbs. Season chops with salt and pepper to taste; rub lightly with flour. Melt remaining 1 tablespoon oil in large skillet over medium heat. Add chops; cook until lightly browned on each side, turning once. Remove chops from skillet to 13 × 9-inch baking dish; cover chops with bread crumb mixture. Top each chop with 1 apple half, cut-side down. Cover dish with foil. Bake 45 minutes or until chops are done and apples are tender.

Applesauce Pork Chops

6 pork chops, 1-inch thick
1 Tbs. oil
1 large onion, cut into thick slices
2 cups applesauce
¾ cup ketchup
½ cup water
⅓ cup vinegar
3 Tbs. brown sugar
2 Tbs. hot pepper sauce
1 Tbs. Worcestershire sauce
Salt and pepper, to taste

Preheat oven to 350°F. Cook chops in hot oil in large skillet just until browned on both sides, turning once; drain. Arrange chops in 13 × 9-inch baking dish; top with onions. Mix applesauce, ketchup, water, vinegar, sugar, pepper sauce, and Worcestershire sauce; season with salt and pepper to taste. Spoon over onions. Cover tightly with foil. Bake 45 minutes to 1 hour or until chops are done.

Eckert's® Apple Burgers

2 links Eckert's Applewurst fresh sausage
1 lb. ground chuck
6 Eckert's® Hamburger Buns

Preheat grill to medium-high heat. Snip ends off sausage links; squeeze meat out of casing into small bowl. Add ground chuck; mix lightly. Shape into 6 patties. Grill 4 to 5 minutes per side or until cooked through. Meanwhile, grill or toast buns. Place burgers in buns. Top with condiments, if desired. Makes 6 servings.

—— *From Our Family Album* ——

Eckert's® Apple Burgers are often found at family birthday celebrations. Mini burgers, or sliders, are the perfect size for kids!

Apple Butter Pork Chops

6 boneless pork chops
1 cup Eckert's® Apple Butter
½ tsp. dried sage leaves
1 tsp. salt
2 large Fuji or Jonagold apples, peeled, cored, and quartered

Place chops in 3-4 quart slow cooker. Mix apple butter, sage, and salt in small bowl. Pour over chops; top with apples. Cover with lid. Cook on low 4 to 6 hours (or on high 2 to 2½ hours). Internal temperature of pork should be 140°F or higher. Serve over couscous or rice, if desired.

Blue Cheese, Apple, and Walnut Steak Spread

1 pkg. (8 oz.) cream cheese, softened
4 oz. crumbled blue cheese
2 Tbs. walnuts, chopped
1 sweet apple, peeled, cored, and sliced

Mix cream cheese and blue cheese in small bowl with electric mixer on low speed until mixture is well blended and smooth. Stir in nuts. Top steaks with a few apple slices. Top apples with teaspoonful of cheese mixture.

Pork Tenderloin with Sautéed Apples and Onions

2 pork tenderloins (1 pound each)
2 Tbs. olive oil
Coarsely ground salt and pepper
1 Vidalia onion, cut in wedges
3 apples, cut in ¼-inch-thick slices
1 Tbs. honey
1 tsp. red wine vinegar

Preheat broiler. Brush tenderloin with 1 tablespoon of olive oil; season with salt and pepper. Broil, 4 inches from heat, 12 to 14 minutes or until tenderloin is done. Meanwhile, heat remaining 1 tablespoon of oil in large skillet over medium heat. Add onions; cook 6 minutes or until tender, stirring occasionally. Stir in apples; cook 3 to 4 minutes or until apples just begin to soften. Remove skillet from heat; stir in honey and vinegar. Season mixture with salt and pepper to taste. Transfer tenderloin to cutting board; cut into thin slices. Serve tenderloin with apple mixture.

—— *From Our Kitchen* ——

To remove the casing from sausage links, snip off the end of the link with a kitchen shears. Over a bowl, squeeze sausage out of the casing by applying pressure to the end opposite of the cut (this is similar to squeezing toothpaste from a tube).

Apple-Stuffed Pork Tenderloin

STUFFING

2 Tbs. butter

2 apples, peeled, cored, and chopped

1 onion, chopped

1 cup fresh bread crumbs

1 tsp. dried oregano leaves

TENDERLOIN

1 pork tenderloin (about 1 lb.)

½ tsp. black pepper

½ tsp. salt

1 Tbs. olive oil

GLAZE

¼ cup maple syrup

2 Tbs. brown sugar

2 Tbs. cider vinegar

1 Tbs. brown mustard

TO PREPARE STUFFING: Melt butter in large skillet over medium heat. Add apples and onions; cook and stir 5 minutes or until onions are light brown and soft. Stir in bread crumbs and oregano. Remove from heat; set aside.

TO PREPARE TENDERLOIN: Preheat oven to 375°F. Place tenderloin on cutting board. Starting at thicker end, make lengthwise cut down center of tenderloin, cutting two-thirds of the way through thickness of meat, adjusting depth of cut as tenderloin tapers, being careful to not cut all the way through to opposite side. Pound tenderloin with meat mallet to ½-inch thickness. Season inside of tenderloin with salt and pepper; cover with stuffing. Roll up tenderloin tightly, starting at one of the long sides; tie with string at 1½-inch intervals. Heat same skillet over medium heat. Add oil and tenderloin. Brown tenderloin on all sides, turning occasionally. Place in 13 × 9-inch baking dish.

TO PREPARE GLAZE: Mix maple syrup, sugar, vinegar, and mustard. Brush about ¼ of glaze over tenderloin.

Bake 45 minutes or until done, brushing with glaze every 15 minutes. Let stand 10 minutes. Remove and discard string before serving. Serve with apple sauce and mashed potatoes, if desired.

Pork with Apple Cream Sauce

1 pork tenderloin (about 1¼ lbs.)
Salt and pepper
1 Tbs. oil
3 Tbs. butter, divided
1 Tbs. flour
¾ cup chicken broth
¾ cup light or heavy cream
½ cup roasted apple sauce (recipe follows)

Cut tenderloin into 1-inch-thick slices. Pound each slice with back of a skillet to ¼-inch thickness; season with salt and pepper to taste. Heat oil and 1 tablespoon of the butter in large skillet over medium heat. Add tenderloin; cook just until cooked through, turning once. Remove tenderloin from skillet; cover to keep warm. Drain skillet. Add 3 tablespoons of chicken broth to skillet; cook on medium heat, stirring to scrape up browned bits from bottom of skillet. Add remaining 2 tablespoons butter. When butter is melted, stir in flour. Cook 1 minute or until broth mixture bubbles, stirring constantly. Slowly add remaining broth, stirring constantly with whisk until mixture is well blended and slightly thickened. Stir in cream, roasted apple sauce, and additional salt and pepper to taste. Continue cooking until sauce thickens. Serve sauce over tenderloin. Makes 4 servings.

Roasted Apple Sauce

1 medium apple, peeled, cored, sliced (about 1¼ cups)
1 to 2 Tbs. olive oil
¼ cup pure maple syrup
¼ cup apple cider vinegar
1 tsp. Dijon mustard
½ tsp. ground sage
¼ tsp. freshly ground black pepper
2 to 3 Tbs. dry Riesling wine (or any dry white wine)
2 Tbs. brown sugar
½ large onion, finely chopped
1 tsp. garlic, minced
½-1 tsp. salt

Preheat oven to 350°F. Toss apple slices with olive oil. Place apple slices in a 9-inch pie plate, and roast until tender about 12 to 15 minutes. Remove from oven and cool. Finely chop roasted apple slices. Combine all ingredients in a 1- or 2-quart saucepan. Bring to a boil over medium-high heat. Reduce to medium-low; simmer uncovered until mixture slightly thickens about 15 to 20 minutes. Cool. Refrigerate in an air-tight container. Bring to room temperature before serving. (Excellent on pork or chicken.) Makes about ⅔ cup.

Pork Sausage and Baked Apples

1 tsp. butter

6 Golden Delicious apples, sliced into ¼-inch rings

1 lb. bulk pork sausage

½ of a yellow onion, finely chopped

⅓ cup firmly packed brown sugar

1 egg, slightly beaten

Preheat oven to 350°F. Grease bottom of 9-inch baking dish with butter. Arrange apples in bottom of dish. Bake 6 minutes. Meanwhile, in a skillet, cook sausage and onion until sausage is no longer pink; drain. Spoon into medium bowl. Add brown sugar and egg; stir to combine. Spoon sausage mixture over baked apples. Bake an additional 8 minutes or until apples are tender.

Sweet Potato Squares
with Lemon-Garlic Mayonnaise

SWEET POTATO SQUARES

2 lbs. sweet potatoes, peeled, cut into 32 (1-inch) cubes

2 Tbs. olive oil

½ tsp. pepper

¼ tsp. salt

½ lb. spicy smoked sausage, cut into 32 (½-inch) pieces

32 wooden toothpicks

MAYONNAISE

1 cup mayonnaise

2 Tbs. fresh flat-leaf parsley, chopped

2 tsp. minced garlic

1 tsp. lemon zest

2 Tbs. fresh lemon juice

½ tsp. pepper

¼ tsp. salt

TO PREPARE SWEET POTATO SQUARES:
Preheat oven to 450°F. Arrange potatoes in single layer on lightly greased 15 × 10 × 1-inch shallow baking pan (jelly roll pan). Drizzle potatoes with oil; sprinkle with pepper and salt. Toss to coat. Bake 15 to 20 minutes or until potatoes are tender, turning every 5 minutes. Meanwhile, cook sausage in large nonstick skillet over medium-high heat 3 to 4 minutes on each side or until browned on both sides, turning once; drain on paper towels. Insert toothpick or small skewer through 1 sausage slice and 1 potato cube. Repeat with remaining sausage slices and potato squares.

TO PREPARE MAYONNAISE: Mix mayonnaise, parsley, garlic, lemon zest and juice, pepper, and salt until well blended. Serve with sweet potato squares.

Pork Tenderloin with Apple Cider Reduction

2 pork tenderloins (about 1 lb. each)
Vegetable oil
Salt and freshly ground black pepper
1½ cups Eckert's® Apple Cider
½ cup apple cider vinegar
¼ cup maple syrup

Move oven rack to lower third of oven; preheat oven to 500°F. Cut each tenderloin crosswise in half; pat tenderloin dry using paper towels. Brush tenderloin with oil; season to taste with salt and pepper. Heat large skillet over medium-high heat. Cook tenderloin, 2 pieces at a time, for 4 minutes or until tenderloin is brown on all sides, turning occasionally. Place tenderloin on shallow baking pan. Bake 15 minutes or until tenderloin is done. Meanwhile, add apple cider and vinegar to same skillet over high heat, stirring to scrape up any browned bits. Cook 8 minutes or until mixture is reduced by two-thirds. Reduce heat to medium; stir in syrup. Remove from heat. Remove tenderloin from baking pan to cutting board; cover with foil. Let stand 5 minutes. Add tenderloin to skillet; spoon sauce over pork. Slice tenderloin into thin slices. Spoon sauce over slices.

—— *From Our Kitchen* ——

Eckert's® Apple Cider is only made during apple season with a blend of Eckert's apples. To preserve cider for use outside of the fall season, pour out about 1 inch of cider from the jug. Recap and freeze cider in the jug. Thaw in the refrigerator. For access to smaller amounts, pour cider into ice-cube trays. Thaw as needed.

Pork Chops and Sweet Potatoes

¾ cup flour

Salt and pepper, to taste

1 lb. boneless pork loin chops, 1-inch thick

2 tsp. vegetable oil

4 sweet potatoes or yams, cooked, cut into pieces

½ cup currant or grape jelly

½ cup orange juice

Grated peel and 1 Tbs. juice from 1 lemon

1 Tbs. unsalted butter

1 tsp. ground mustard

1 tsp. paprika

½ tsp. ground ginger

Preheat oven to 350°F. Mix flour with salt and pepper in shallow dish. Add chops, one at a time, to coat. Heat oil in heavy nonstick skillet on medium-high heat. Add chops; cook until browned on both sides, turning once. Place chops in 13 × 9-inch baking dish; add sweet potatoes. Combine orange juice, jelly, lemon zest and juice, butter, mustard, paprika, and ginger in small saucepan. Bring to boil; simmer 3 minutes, stirring occasionally. Pour ¾ cup of the sauce over potatoes in dish. Bake 40 to 45 minutes or until chops are done, brushing occasionally with remaining sauce.

Microwave Spaghetti Squash

1 spaghetti squash (1½ lbs.)

1 red pepper, thinly sliced

1 small onion, thinly sliced

2 cloves garlic, minced

1 Tbs. olive oil

1 tomato, chopped

1 zucchini, thinly sliced

1 cup mushrooms, sliced

1 Tbs. tarragon vinegar

1 tsp. dried tarragon

½ tsp. salt

¼ tsp. black pepper

Pierce whole squash several times with fork; place in glass baking dish. Microwave on high 9 minutes or until squash is soft, turning squash after 5 minutes. Let stand 5 minutes. Cut squash lengthwise in half; remove and discard seeds. Pull out squash strands from shells using fork. Place squash in large serving bowl; cover to keep warm. Combine red peppers, onions, garlic, and oil in medium casserole dish; cover. Microwave on high 2 minutes or until vegetables are crisp-tender. Add tomato, zucchini, mushrooms, vinegar, tarragon, salt, and pepper; toss to combine. Cover; microwave on high 3 minutes or until zucchini is crisp-tender. Toss red pepper mixture with squash strands. Makes 6 to 8 servings.

Herbed Spaghetti Squash with Mozzarella

1 large spaghetti squash (about 3 lbs.), halved lengthwise, seeded

¼ cup unsalted butter; cut in bits

5 large cloves garlic, cut in half

Salt and pepper

1 cup packed basil leaves, finely shredded

4 oz. smoked or plain mozzarella, cut into ¼-inch cubes

Freshly grated Parmesan cheese (optional)

Preheat oven to 375°F. Place squash cut-sides up in 13 × 9-inch baking pan; fill centers with butter and garlic. Season with ½ teaspoon salt and ¼ teaspoon pepper; cover tightly with foil. Bake 1½ hours or until squash is very tender. Remove garlic to small bowl; mash with fork. Pull out squash strands from shells using fork; place squash in large bowl. Add mashed garlic, basil, and cheese; toss to combine. Season to taste with additional salt and pepper. Sprinkle with freshly grated Parmesan cheese.

Baked Spaghetti Squash with Garlic and Butter

1 spaghetti squash

2 Tbs. butter

2 cloves garlic, minced

¼ cup minced parsley or basil

½ tsp. kosher salt

¼ cup grated Parmesan cheese

Preheat oven to 375°F. Place squash in baking pan; bake 1 hour or until squash is tender when pierced with knife. Cool 15 minutes. Cut lengthwise in half; remove and discard seeds. Pull out squash strands from shells using fork. Heat large skillet over medium heat. Add butter and garlic; cook and stir until garlic begins to brown and becomes fragrant. Add squash strands, parsley, and salt; toss to combine. Sprinkle with cheese. Cook until squash is slightly crunchy and cheese begins to melt, stirring constantly.

Butternut Squash Pasta

1 small butternut squash, seeded, cut into quarters
½ cup water
1¾ cup flour
1 tsp. hazelnut butter
Dash of garlic powder
Dash of black pepper
Dash of ground nutmeg

Preheat oven to 350°F. Place squash and water in 8-inch square baking dish; cover with foil. Bake 50 minutes to 1 hour or until squash is tender. Remove from oven; cool. Mash flesh; measure mashed squash to get ¾ cup. (Any extra squash can be frozen for another use.) Mix squash with flour, hazelnut butter, garlic powder, pepper, and nutmeg to form soft dough. Knead dough on lightly floured surface until dough is soft and pliable. (Dough will be a similar texture to bread dough.) Place dough in bowl; cover with plastic wrap. Let stand 30 minutes. Shape dough into desired pasta shape(s) and cook as desired.

—— *From Our Kitchen* ——

Cook squash in your microwave for faster preparation. Pierce the whole squash several times with fork; place in glass baking dish. Microwave on high for 18 minutes, turn squash every 3-4 minutes. Let stand 5 minutes. Microwave butter in small microwavable bowl on high for 30 seconds or until butter is melted. Add garlic; cook on high for 1 minute. Mash garlic with fork. Cut squash lengthwise in half; remove seeds. Continue as directed in recipe.

Acorn-Cabbage Bake

2 large acorn squash
1 Tbs. butter
2 cups shredded cabbage
1 onion, chopped
1 apple, chopped
½ lb. pork sausage, cooked, drained
2 Tbs. slivered almonds
¾ tsp. salt
½ tsp. ground sage
¼ tsp. ground thyme
¼ tsp. pepper

Preheat oven to 400°F. Cut squash lengthwise in half; remove and discard seeds. Add ½ inch of water to 13 × 9-inch baking dish. Place squash, cut-sides down, in dish. Bake 20 minutes or until squash is tender; cool 15 minutes. Pull out squash strands from shells using fork and set aside. Reduce oven temperature to 350°F. Melt butter in large skillet; add cabbage, onions, and apples. Cook and stir 5 minutes or until vegetables are tender. Add meat, nuts, salt, sage, thyme, and pepper; mix well. Stir in squash. Spoon mixture into greased 2-quart casserole dish. Bake 30 minutes or until heated through. Makes 8 servings.

Cider-Flavored Chicken

1 pint dry (hard) apple cider
2 boneless skinless chicken breast halves
½ tsp. salt
½ tsp. ground allspice
2 Tbs. butter
2 apples, peeled, chopped
3 stalks celery, sliced
½ lb. mushrooms, sliced
¼ cup heavy whipping cream

Bring cider to boil in saucepan; continue cooking until liquid has reduced by half. Meanwhile, rub chicken with salt and allspice. Melt 1 tablespoon of the butter in medium skillet. Add apples and celery; cook until apples are golden brown, stirring occasionally. Remove apple mixture; set aside. Add remaining 1 tablespoon butter to same skillet; cook until butter is melted. Add chicken; cook until browned on both sides, turning once. Add cider mixture; bring to boil. Stir in celery. Reduce heat to medium-low; simmer 30 minutes or until chicken is done, stirring occasionally and adding apple mixture for the last 5 minutes. Remove chicken from skillet; stir in cream. Cook until heated through. Serve sauce over chicken.

Beef Pot Roast
with Maple Potatoes and Cider Gravy

1 Tbs. vegetable oil

1 boneless beef chuck shoulder roast (about 3 lbs.)

1 cup onions, chopped

2 tsp. chopped fresh or 1 tsp. dried thyme

1¼ tsp. salt, divided

¾ tsp. pepper, divided

1 cup beef broth

¾ cup + 2 Tbs. Eckert's® Apple Cider, divided

3 lbs. sweet potatoes, peeled, cut into 1-inch pieces

4 cloves garlic

2 Tbs. maple syrup

1 tsp. minced fresh ginger (optional)

2 Tbs. cornstarch

Heat oil in Dutch oven or large saucepan over medium heat. Add meat; brown on all sides, turning occasionally. Remove beef; set aside. Drain drippings from pan. Add onions, thyme, 1 teaspoon of salt, and ½ teaspoon of pepper; cook and stir 3 to 5 minutes or until onion is tender. Stir in broth and ¾ cup of the cider. Increase heat to medium-high; cook 2 minutes, stirring to scrape brown bits from bottom of pot. Return beef to pot. Bring to boil; reduce heat to medium-low. Cover; simmer 2½ hours or until meat is tender. Add potatoes and garlic; continue simmering 30 minutes or until potatoes are tender. Remove meat; cover to keep warm. Remove potatoes and garlic to large bowl using slotted spoon. Add maple syrup, ginger, remaining ¼ teaspoon salt, and remaining ¼ teaspoon pepper to potatoes. Beat potato mixture with electric mixer on low until potatoes are mashed and mixture is smooth; cover to keep warm. Dissolve cornstarch in remaining 2 tablespoons apple cider. Skim fat from cooking liquid; stir in cornstarch mixture. Bring to boil, stirring constantly. Cook and stir 1 minute or until liquid is thickened. Cut meat into slices; serve with mashed potatoes and pan gravy.

—— *From Our Kitchen* ——

A beef top or bottom round roast can be substituted for the chuck roast.

Bratwurst Stew

4 cups green cabbage (about ½ head), coarsely chopped

1 lb. Eckert's® Bratwurst, cut into 1-inch-thick slices

1½ cups cubed red potatoes

¾ cup red peppers, chopped

1 onion, cut in half, then into thin wedges

3½ cups chicken broth

1 Tbs. Eckert's® Hot & Sharp Mustard

1 Tbs. cider vinegar

¼ tsp. salt

¼ tsp. ground black pepper

⅛ tsp. celery seed

Combine cabbage, meat, potatoes, red peppers, and onions in a 5-quart slow cooker. Mix broth, mustard, vinegar, salt, black pepper, and celery seed with wire whisk until well blended; pour over cabbage mixture. Cover with lid. Cook on low 6 to 8 hours (or on high 3 to 3½ hours). Makes 6 servings.

From Our Kitchen

To prepare this recipe on the stovetop, substitute a Dutch oven or large saucepan for the slow cooker. Bring stew to boil; reduce heat and simmer 1 hour, stirring occasionally.

Chicken Vegetable Stew

4 small boneless skinless chicken breast halves (¾ to 1 lb.)

4 skinless bone-in chicken thighs

3 to 5 Tbs. oil, divided

1 large zucchini, finely chopped (approx. 2 cups zucchini)

8 oz. fresh mushrooms, sliced (optional)

1 onion, finely chopped

½ cup green pepper, finely chopped

½ cup red pepper, finely chopped

2 to 3 cloves garlic, minced

4 Roma tomatoes, finely chopped

2 Tbs. concentrated tomato paste

1½ cups water

1 tsp. dried thyme leaves

1 tsp. oregano leaves

1 tsp. dried marjoram leaves

1 tsp. dried basil leaves

Cut chicken breasts into 1-inch cubes; cook in 1 to 2 tablespoons hot oil in large cast iron skillet or heavy bottom skillet until chicken is browned on all sides, stirring occasionally. Remove from skillet to 3-quart slow cooker. Add 1 to 2 tablespoons of the remaining oil to same skillet. Add chicken thighs. Cook until browned on both sides, turning once; transfer to slow cooker. Add zucchini, mushrooms, onion, green and red peppers, and garlic; spoon over chicken in slow cooker. Add tomatoes, tomato paste, water, thyme, oregano, marjoram, and basil. Cover with lid. Cook on low 2 to 3 hours or until vegetables are tender. Season to taste with salt and freshly ground black pepper just before serving, if desired. Makes 6 servings.

Other vegetables can be added, such as green peas, carrots, green beans.

APPLE DESSERTS, BREADS, & MUFFINS

—— *From Our Family Album* ——

Jill and Chris Eckert are seated next to each other on the straw bale in 1975 at Eckert's Millstadt Farm on a busy weekend. Jill and Chris grew up on this farm with their older sister, Sarah. Today Jill is the vice president of Food Service and Marketing and Chris is president of Eckert Companies. Their training program started at an early age.

Apple Smoothie

½ cup Eckert's® Apple Cider
2 scoops Eckert's® Frozen Custard
½ of an apple, chopped

Blend all ingredients in a blender-style food-preparing machine (such as Magic Bullet®) or blender until smooth. Serve immediately.

Apple Cranberry Drink

8 cups Eckert's® Apple Cider, chilled
4 cups cranberry juice, chilled
4 cups ginger ale, chilled
Lemon or lime slices, for garnish

Mix cider, juice, and ginger ale in a punch bowl. Float lemon slices on top for garnish, if desired.

Baked Eckert's® Apples

4 large baking apples (Golden Delicious, Jonathan, or Jonagold)
¼ cup sugar
¼ cup pecans, chopped
¼ cup raisins, chopped
1 tsp. ground cinnamon
1 Tbs. butter
¾ cup boiling water

Preheat oven to 375°F. Remove apple cores to within ½ inch of the bottom of each apple using apple corer, making the holes about ¾-inch wide. Combine sugar, nuts, raisins, and cinnamon. Place apples, top-sides up, in 8-inch square baking dish. Spoon nut mixture evenly into apples. Top each with dot of butter. Carefully pour boiling water into bottom of dish. Bake 30 to 40 minutes or until apples are tender but not mushy. Baste apples with liquid in dish just before serving.

Apple Bread
with Butter-Sugar Topping

BREAD
1 cup sugar
½ cup butter, softened
1 tsp. baking soda
¼ cup buttermilk
2 eggs, lightly beaten
1 tsp. vanilla
2 cups flour
½ tsp. salt
2 cups apples, chopped
½ cup nuts, chopped

TOPPING
2 Tbs. butter, softened
2 Tbs. sugar
2 Tbs. flour
½ tsp. ground cinnamon

TO PREPARE BREAD: Preheat oven to 350°F. Beat sugar and butter in large bowl with electric mixer until well blended. Stir baking soda into buttermilk. Add to sugar mixture; mix well. Blend in eggs and vanilla. Add flour and salt; mix well. Gently stir in apples and nuts. Pour into greased and floured 9 × 5-inch loaf pan. Drop teaspoonfuls of butter-sugar topping over batter. Bake 50 minutes or until wooden toothpick inserted in center of loaf comes out clean. Cool in pan 10 minutes before removing to wire rack.

TO PREPARE TOPPING: Mix butter, sugar, flour, and cinnamon. Drop by teaspoonfuls over apple bread before baking as directed.

—— *From Our Kitchen* ——

Make your own buttermilk by pouring one tablespoon of white vinegar or lemon juice in a liquid measuring cup. Add enough milk to bring the liquid up to the one-cup line. Let stand for five minutes. Then use as much as is called for in the recipe.

Apple Muffins

1 egg, lightly beaten
⅔ cup sugar
¼ cup butter or margarine, melted
½ tsp. salt
½ tsp. ground cinnamon
¼ tsp. ground nutmeg
1 cup milk
1 tsp. lemon juice
½ tsp. vanilla
2 cups flour
3 tsp. baking powder
1 cup apples, chopped
½ cup raisins or chopped nuts (optional)

Preheat oven to 400°F. Beat egg, butter, sugar, salt, cinnamon, and nutmeg in medium bowl with electric mixer until light and fluffy. Stir in milk, juice, and vanilla. In small bowl, mix flour and baking powder. Stir flour mixture into sugar mixture just until blended. Gently stir in apples and raisins. Spoon into greased muffin cups, filling each ⅔ full. Bake for 25 minutes or until wooden toothpick inserted in center of muffin comes out clean.

From Our Farm

When our great-great-grandfather planted apple trees, they grew 25 feet high and 30 feet wide. Our most recent plantings are now as close as three feet apart and will reach 12 feet in height. Although smaller in stature, today's trees will be five times as productive per acre. They also bear fruit seven years earlier!

Chunky Apple Muffin with Caramel Sauce

MUFFIN
2 large apples, chopped
2 tsp. lemon zest
4 tsp. fresh lemon juice
1 cup butter, softened
2 cups sugar
3 eggs
1 tsp. vanilla
3 cups flour
1½ tsp. baking soda
½ tsp. salt
1 cup pecans, chopped

SAUCE
1 cup sugar
½ cup water
¾ cup whipping cream
1 Tbs. butter

TO PREPARE MUFFIN: Preheat oven to 325°F. Combine apples, lemon zest, and juice; set aside. Beat butter until fluffy in large bowl with electric mixer. Gradually beat in sugar. Add eggs and vanilla; beat well. Mix in flour, baking soda, and salt until well blended. Gently stir in apple mixture and nuts. Pour into greased and floured fluted tube pan (such as a Bundt® pan). Bake 1 hour and 15 minutes or until wooden toothpick inserted near center of cake comes out clean. Cool in pan 10 minutes, then remove from pan to wire rack. Serve caramel sauce over warm cake slices.

TO PREPARE SAUCE: Mix sugar and water in heavy saucepan; bring to boil over medium-high heat. Reduce heat to medium; cook 15 minutes, without stirring, until sugar mixture is amber (dark orange-yellow) color. (Do not let sugar mixture get too brown.) Remove from heat; let stand 2 minutes to cool slightly. Gradually stir in cream. Add butter; stir until mixture is well blended. To serve, cook caramel sauce on medium heat until sauce is heated through and smooth.

Stacked Apple "Pies" with Eckert's® Vanilla Custard and Caramel Sauce

CRUST

1 frozen Eckert's® Pie Crust, thawed

1 Tbs. unsalted butter, melted

2 Tbs. coarse granulated sugar (such as Sugar in the Raw®)

CREAMY CARAMEL SAUCE

1 cup sugar

¼ cup warm water

2 Tbs. corn syrup

Pinch of salt

½ cup heavy cream

1 Tbs. dark rum (optional)

½ stick unsalted butter

1 tsp. vanilla

APPLE FILLING

1 Tbs. unsalted butter

2 Jonathan apples, peeled, cored, and thinly sliced

1 Granny Smith apple, peeled, cored, and thinly sliced

½ cup golden raisins

¼ tsp. ground cinnamon

Pinch of salt

½ cup Eckert's® Apple Cider

Creamy caramel sauce

Eckert's® Frozen Custard

TO PREPARE CRUST: Preheat oven to 400°F. Line baking sheet with parchment paper. Unroll pie crust onto prepared baking sheet. Brush crust with melted butter; sprinkle with sugar. Cut dough into 12 wedges using pastry wheel or pizza cutter. Bake 15 minutes or until crisp and golden. Remove from oven; cool completely.

TO PREPARE SAUCE: Bring sugar, water, corn syrup, and salt to boil in small saucepan over medium-high heat, swirling occasionally. Continue cooking 10 minutes or until mixture is the color of iced tea. Gradually add cream and rum while stirring constantly with whisk. Remove from heat; stir in butter and vanilla. Pour sauce into heatproof bowl to cool. Makes about 1 cup.

TO PREPARE APPLE FILLING: Meanwhile, melt butter in nonstick skillet over medium heat; add apples, raisins, cinnamon, and salt. Cook and stir 4 minutes or until apples begin to soften. Add cider; simmer on medium-low until almost all liquid has evaporated, stirring constantly. Stir in ¾ cup of the creamy caramel sauce. Reduce heat to low to keep apple mixture warm. To serve: Place 1 crust wedge on each of 6 individual serving plates. Top each with 2 small scoops of frozen custard, a spoonful of apple mixture, and about 2 teaspoonfuls of caramel sauce. Cover with remaining crust wedges, ice cream, and apple mixture. Serve immediately. Makes 6 servings. Pie wedges may be baked up to 2 days before serving. Store in airtight container.

Apple Crumb Pie

5 cups apples, sliced, peeled
1 (9-inch) unbaked pie shell
1 cup sugar, divided
1 tsp. ground cinnamon
¾ cup flour
⅓ cup cold butter

Preheat oven to 450°F. Arrange apples in bottom of pie shell. Mix ½ cup of the sugar with cinnamon; sprinkle over apples. Mix remaining ½ cup sugar and the flour in small bowl; cut in butter with pastry blender or 2 knives until mixture forms pea-sized crumbs. Sprinkle over apple mixture. Bake 10 minutes. Reduce oven temperature to 350°F and bake an additional 30 minutes or until apples are tender.

—— *From Our Kitchen* ——

The Eckert family "secret" to the best-tasting apple pie is to use a ratio of 4 Jonathan apples for every Golden Delicious apple.

Apple Cream Pie

FILLING
1 egg
1 cup sour cream
¾ cup sugar
½ tsp. vanilla
2 Tbs. flour
4 cups apples, sliced, peeled
1 (10-inch) unbaked pie shell

TOPPING
½ cup flour
¼ cup butter, softened
½ tsp. ground cinnamon

TO PREPARE FILLING: Preheat oven to 400°F. Beat egg, sour cream, sugar, and vanilla in a large bowl with wire whisk until well blended. Stir in flour. Add apples; mix lightly. Carefully spoon into pie shell. Bake 15 minutes. Reduce oven temperature to 325°F and bake an additional 30 minutes.

TO PREPARE TOPPING: Meanwhile, mix flour, butter, and cinnamon. Remove pie from oven; sprinkle with topping. Bake an additional 15 minutes.

Eckert's® Golden Delicious Apple Pie

6 to 7 cups Golden Delicious apples, sliced
1 cup sugar
6 Tbs. whipping cream (optional)
1 Tbs. flour
1 Tbs. butter or margarine, melted
Dash of ground cinnamon or ground nutmeg
1 Tbs. milk
2 (9-inch) unbaked pie crusts

Preheat oven to 425°F. Combine apples, sugar, whipping cream, flour, butter, and cinnamon. Place 1 of the pie crusts in 9-inch pie plate. Fill with apple mixture. Cover with remaining crust; seal and flute edge. Prick top crust with fork several times to allow steam to escape. Brush crust with milk. Bake at 425°F for 15 minutes. Reduce oven temperature to 350°F; bake an additional 45 minutes.

Apple Pie in a Glass

¼ cup sugar
¼ cup water
Pinch of ground cinnamon
3 large tart apples (such as Granny Smith), peeled, cored, and chopped
16 shortbread cookies, crumbled
1 pint vanilla ice cream

Mix sugar, water, and cinnamon in medium saucepan; add apples. Cook, covered, over medium heat for 15 minutes, stirring occasionally. Remove lid; cook an additional 10 minutes or until all liquid has evaporated, stirring constantly. Spoon half of the cookie crumbs evenly into 4 dessert glasses. Spoon ice cream over crumbs. Top with warm apple mixture and remaining crumbs. Makes 4 servings.

Baked Cranberry Apples

4 Golden Delicious or Jonathan apples
2 cups fresh cranberries
¾ cup orange juice
¼ cup raisins
¼ cup honey
2 Tbs. butter, melted
½ tsp. orange zest
½ tsp. ground nutmeg
½ tsp. vanilla
4 whole cinnamon sticks

Preheat oven to 350°F. Slice ½ inch off top of each apple, including stem, to create a "lid." Remove stem from each "lid"; cut out a small hole using paring knife big enough to hold a cinnamon stick. Core the bottom of each apple using melon baller, being careful not to cut through bottom of apple. Scoop out the inside of each apple with melon baller, being careful not to pierce the skin. Chop removed apple flesh; place in medium bowl. Add cranberries, juice, raisins, honey, butter, zest, nutmeg, and vanilla; toss to combine. Spoon apple mixture evenly into hollowed-out apple shells; place apples in greased baking dish. Replace "lid" on each apple, inserting 1 cinnamon stick through each stem hole. Spoon any extra stuffing around apples in dish. Bake 45 minutes or until apples are tender.

Fresh Apple Pastry

PASTRY

2½ cups all-purpose flour + 2 Tbs.

1 cup vegetable shortening (1 Crisco baking stick)

1 Tbs. granulated sugar

1 tsp. salt

1 large egg, separated

⅔ cup milk

1 cup crushed corn flakes (2½ cups, uncrushed)

8 to 9 large apples, peeled, cored, and ¼-inch sliced (Baker needs to cover the bottom pastry with apple slices)

¾ cup granulated sugar

1 Tbs. all-purpose flour

1 tsp. ground cinnamon

GLAZE

2 Tbs. milk

1 cup powdered sugar

Preheat oven to 375°F. Mix flour, shortening, sugar, and salt until well blended. Place egg yolk in a liquid 1-cup measuring cup; add milk to measure ⅔ cup. Beat egg and milk; add to flour mixture. Mix well. Divide pastry dough in half. Roll out one pastry dough piece into 15 × 10-inch rectangle on lightly floured surface. Carefully transfer pastry into ungreased 15 × 10 × 1-inch baking pan (jelly roll pan). Sprinkle pastry with corn flakes; arrange apples on top. Mix granulated sugar, flour, and cinnamon; sprinkle over apples.

Roll out remaining pastry into 15 × 10-inch rectangle on lightly floured surface. Carefully transfer pastry to cover apples in pan. Beat egg white lightly; brush over top pastry. Bake in preheated oven for 45 minutes. Then reduce heat to 350°F for 15 minutes or until golden brown. Cool on wire rack until warm but not cool. Drizzle glaze on warm pastry. Cut into 2 × 2-inch squares. Makes about 35.

Glazed Apple Cake

CAKE

2 eggs
1 cup granulated sugar
¼ cup butter, softened
1 cup flour
2 tsp. baking powder
½ tsp. salt
½ tsp. ground cinnamon
½ tsp. allspice
2 cups apples, finely chopped
1 cup nuts, chopped

GLAZE

1 cup powdered sugar
2 Tbs. milk
½ tsp. vanilla

TO PREPARE CAKE: Preheat oven to 350°F. Beat eggs in medium bowl with wire whisk. Add granulated sugar; beat until well blended and thick. Mix in butter. Combine flour, baking powder, salt, cinnamon, and allspice. Add to egg mixture; mix until well blended. Gently stir in apples and nuts. Pour into greased and floured 8-inch square baking pan. Bake 45 minutes to 1 hour or until wooden toothpick inserted in center of cake comes out clean. Cool completely in pan on wire rack.

TO PREPARE GLAZE: Meanwhile, mix powdered sugar, milk, and vanilla until smooth. Spread over warm cake.

Eckert's® Easiest Apple Cake

2 eggs
1½ cups sugar
1 cup flour
2 tsp. baking powder
½ tsp. salt
2 cups apples, finely chopped
1 cup pecans, chopped

Preheat oven to 350°F. Beat eggs and sugar in large bowl with electric mixer until well blended and thick. Combine flour, baking powder, and salt. Add to egg mixture; beat well. Gently stir in apples and nuts. Pour into greased 8-inch square baking pan. Bake 55 to 60 minutes or until wooden toothpick inserted in center of cake comes out clean. Cool completely in pan on wire rack. Serve plain or with vanilla ice cream or custard.

Apple-Walnut Cake
with Cream Cheese Frosting

CAKE

2 large eggs
1⅔ cups sugar
½ cup vegetable oil
2 tsp. vanilla
2 cups flour
2 tsp. baking soda
1½ tsp. ground cinnamon
1 tsp. salt
½ tsp. ground nutmeg
5 large apples, peeled and chopped
1 cup walnuts, coarsely chopped

FROSTING

6 oz. cream cheese, softened
3 Tbs. butter
1 tsp. vanilla
1½ cups powdered sugar

TO PREPARE CAKE: Preheat oven to 350°F. Beat eggs and sugar with electric mixer in large bowl until well blended. Add oil and vanilla; mix well. Combine flour, baking soda, cinnamon, salt, and nutmeg. Gradually add to egg mixture, beating well after each addition. Gently stir in apples and nuts. Pour into a greased and floured 13 × 9-inch baking pan. Bake 50 to 55 minutes or until wooden toothpick inserted in center of cake comes out clean. Cool completely in pan on wire rack. Frost with cream cheese frosting. Store frosted cake in refrigerator.

TO PREPARE FROSTING: Beat cream cheese, butter, and vanilla in small mixing bowl with wire whisk until well blended. Gradually beat in sugar until desired consistency is reached.

Spicy Apple Bars

BARS

¼ cup butter

1 cup firmly packed brown sugar

1 egg, lightly beaten

½ cup strong brewed hot coffee

1½ cups flour

1 tsp. baking powder

¼ tsp. baking soda

½ tsp. salt

½ tsp. ground cinnamon

Dash of cloves

2 cups apples, finely chopped

½ cup nuts

FROSTING

2 cups powdered sugar

2 Tbs. butter, softened

2 Tbs. milk

1 tsp. vanilla

TO PREPARE BARS: Preheat oven to 350°F. Mix shortening and brown sugar until well blended. Stir in coffee and egg. Combine flour, baking powder, baking soda, salt, cinnamon, and cloves. Add to shortening mixture; mix well. Gently stir in apples and nuts. Pour mixture into greased 13 × 9-inch baking pan. Bake 18 to 20 minutes or until wooden toothpick inserted in center comes out clean. Cool completely in pan on wire rack.

TO PREPARE FROSTING: Mix powdered sugar, butter, milk, and vanilla until well blended. Frost bars while still warm. Cut into bars to serve.

Slow Cooked Apples

7 large apples (such as Golden Delicious or Jonathan), peeled, cored, and quartered (approx. 8 cups)

½ cup orange juice

⅓ cup sugar

1 tsp. ground cinnamon

½ cup raisins

Place in a 3-4 quart slow cooker. Mix juice, sugar, and cinnamon in small bowl. Stir in raisins; pour over apples. Stir to coat apples; cover with lid. Cook on low 1 to 2 hours or until apples are tender. Makes 12 (½ cup) servings. Serve with favorite pork recipe.

Apple Goodie
with Oatmeal and Brown Sugar Topping

GOODIE

5 cups apples, pared and sliced
¾ cup sugar
½ tsp. ground cinnamon

TOPPING

¾ cup oatmeal
¾ cup packed brown sugar
¾ cup flour
¼ tsp. baking powder
¼ tsp. baking soda
⅛ tsp. salt
½ cup butter or margarine

TO PREPARE GOODIES: Arrange apples in a 9-inch square baking pan. In a small bowl, mix sugar and cinnamon together; sprinkle over apples and mix well. Spoon oatmeal and brown sugar topping over top of apples and pat firmly. Bake at 400°F for 30 to 40 minutes until a crust is formed. Serve hot or cold. Serve with ice cream. Serves 9.

TO PREPARE TOPPING: In a mixing bowl, combine oatmeal, brown sugar, flour, baking powder, baking soda, and salt; cut in butter and work with fingertips until mixture is crumbly.

—— *From Our Family Album* ——

When Chris was living on the East Coast, he and Angie visited another family apple farm. The owners gave Chris and Angie their favorite apple recipe . . . Apple Goodie. It is now an Eckert family favorite!

Apple-Raisin Bread Pudding

2 cups milk
2 eggs, lightly beaten
1 tsp. vanilla
½ cup granulated sugar
5 large apples, peeled, chopped
10 to 12 slices stale bread, cubed
½ cup golden raisins
½ cup firmly packed brown sugar
¼ cup butter at room temperature, cubed
½ tsp. ground cinnamon
Dash of ground nutmeg (optional)

Preheat oven to 350°F. Mix milk, eggs, and vanilla in medium bowl; stir in granulated sugar. Add apples, bread cubes, and raisins; mix lightly. Pour into 8-inch square baking dish. Combine remaining ingredients; sprinkle over apple mixture. Bake 30 to 40 minutes or until golden brown. Serve warm with caramel ice cream topping or whipping cream, if desired.

Apple Betty

4 cups sliced apples
¼ cup orange juice
¾ cup sugar
¾ cup flour
½ tsp. ground cinnamon
¼ tsp. ground nutmeg
½ cup cold butter
Whipping cream or ice cream

Preheat oven to 350°F. Mound apples in center of buttered 9-inch pie plate or 1½-quart round baking dish; sprinkle with orange juice. Mix sugar, flour, cinnamon, and nutmeg; cut in butter with pastry cutter or 2 knives until mixture resembles coarse crumbs. Sprinkle over apples. Bake 45 minutes or until apples are tender and topping is crisp. Serve warm, topped with whipping cream or ice cream.

Eckert's® Apple Crisp

4 large Golden Delicious apples, peeled and sliced
1 cup sugar, divided
½ cup butter or margarine
¾ cup quick-cooking rolled oats
½ cup flour
½ cup almonds or pecans, chopped
Ice cream (optional)

Preheat oven to 350°F. Combine apples and ½ cup of the sugar in 8-inch square baking pan. Mix butter, oats, flour, remaining ½ cup sugar, and the nuts; sprinkle over apples. Bake 1 hour or until topping is browned and apples are tender. Serve warm topped with ice cream.

Apple Crisp for One

1 apple, peeled, sliced
1 Tbs. flour
1 Tbs. quick-cooking rolled oats
1 Tbs. brown sugar
⅛ tsp. ground cinnamon
1 Tbs. cold margarine

Preheat oven to 350°F. Place slices in small baking dish. Mix flour, oats, sugar, and cinnamon; cut in margarine with pastry cutter or 2 knives until mixture is crumbly. Sprinkle over slices. Bake 25 minutes.

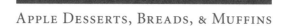
Golden Apple Crisp

4 large Golden Delicious apples, peeled, thinly sliced (about 5 to 6 cups)
½ cup quick-cooking rolled oats
½ cup flour
½ cup butter, softened
¼ cup coconut, shredded
¼ cup pecans, chopped
¼ cup firmly packed brown sugar
½ tsp. ground cinnamon
Ice cream

Preheat oven to 375°F. Arrange apple slices in ungreased 8-inch square baking pan. Combine oats, flour, coconut, nuts, sugar, and cinnamon. Cut in butter with pastry blender or 2 knives until mixture forms large crumbs. Sprinkle evenly over apples. Bake 45 minutes or until apples are tender. Serve warm topped with ice cream.

Cranberry-Apple Crisp with Pecan Topping

CRISP
5 Granny Smith apples, peeled, sliced
1 can (16 oz.) whole cranberry sauce
¾ cup granulated sugar
2 Tbs. flour

TOPPING
1 cup quick-cooking rolled oats
¼ cup packed brown sugar
¼ cup flour
¼ cup pecans or walnuts, chopped
¼ cup butter, melted
1 tsp. ground cinnamon

TO PREPARE CRISP: Preheat oven to 350°F. Arrange apples in 13 × 9-inch baking dish. Combine cranberry sauce, sugar, and flour. Pour over apples in pan; toss lightly to coat. Sprinkle pecan topping evenly over apple mixture. Bake 35 to 40 minutes or until apples are tender. Serve warm with Eckert's® Frozen Custard.

TO PREPARE TOPPING: Combine oats, sugar, flour, nuts, butter, and cinnamon.

Poached Pears with Caramel Sauce

PEARS

2 cups water
½ cup apple cider
½ cup granulated sugar
4 firm ripe pears, peeled, cored
½ tsp. vanilla

CARAMEL SAUCE

½ cup butter
1 cup firmly packed brown sugar
1 can (5 oz.) evaporated milk
1 tsp. vanilla

TO PREPARE PEARS: Mix water, cider, and granulated sugar in large skillet. Bring to boil over medium heat. Reduce heat to medium-low; place pears in skillet, top-sides up. Place a round of wax paper directly on top of the pears to prevent discoloration. Simmer 20 minutes or until pears are tender. Transfer pears to serving plate using slotted spoon; set aside. Increase heat to high; cook the poaching liquid 5 to 10 minutes or until it has been reduced to about ½ cup. Remove from heat; stir in vanilla.

TO PREPARE SAUCE: Melt butter in small saucepan over medium heat; stir in brown sugar and milk. Bring mixture to boil. Remove from heat; stir in vanilla. Spoon half of the caramel sauce evenly into 4 dessert dishes. Place 1 pear in each dish using slotted spoon. Spoon remaining sauce over pears. Makes 4 servings.

Apple Pandowdy

6 tart apples, peeled, sliced
1 cup sugar
½ tsp. ground cinnamon
½ tsp. salt, divided
2 Tbs. butter, softened
1 cup flour
1 tsp. baking powder
2 Tbs. shortening
⅜ cup milk
Whipping cream

Preheat oven to 375°F. Arrange apples in buttered 8-inch square baking dish. Mix sugar, cinnamon, and ¼ teaspoon salt; sprinkle over apples. Dot with butter. Mix flour, baking powder, and remaining ¼ teaspoon of the salt; cut in shortening with pastry blender or 2 knives until mixture forms large crumbs. Add milk; stir until soft dough forms. Roll out dough on lightly floured surface into 8-inch square; place over apples in pan. Bake 35 minutes or until apples are tender and crust is golden brown. Invert into serving dish. Top with dollops of whipping cream when serving.

Port-Poached Pears and Ricotta

2 Anjou or Bosc pears, peeled and cored
2 cups Port wine
¾ cup pure maple syrup
1 cup ricotta cheese

Mix wine and syrup in medium saucepan; add pears. Bring to boil over medium-high heat. Reduce heat to medium-low; cover. Simmer 20 minutes or until pears are tender, turning pears occasionally. Remove from heat; let stand to cool. Remove pears from poaching liquid. Cut a small slice, about ¼-inch thick, from rounded bottom of the pear so it will sit upright; set pears aside. Cook poaching liquid over medium-high heat until it becomes thick and syrupy; remove from heat to cool. Cut each pear vertically in half. Drizzle spoonful of poaching liquid onto 4 individual serving plates; top each with 1 pear half. Spoon ¼ cup cheese into center of each pear. Makes 4 servings.

Apple Fritters

2 cups flour
2 tsp. baking powder
1 tsp. salt
1 cup milk
2 eggs, separated
1 Tbs. sugar
2 cups sliced apples
Oil for frying
Maple syrup or honey (optional)

Mix flour, baking powder, and salt. Heat milk until just warmer than lukewarm. Beat egg yolks with sugar in medium bowl with wire whisk until well blended. Blend in milk. Gradually stir in flour mixture, mixing until well blended. Beat egg whites in small bowl until soft peaks form. Gently stir into egg mixture. Stir in apples. Heat oil to 320°F to 330°F over medium heat. Fry fritters, in batches, by carefully dropping rounded tablespoonfuls of dough into oil. Fry fritters until light brown on both sides, turning once. Serve with maple syrup, if desired.

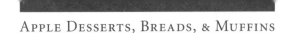
Taffy Apple Pizza

1 pkg. (20 oz.) refrigerated sugar cookie dough

1 pkg. (8 oz.) cream cheese, softened

½ cup firmly packed brown sugar

2 Tbs. creamy peanut butter

1 tsp. vanilla

½ cup water

2 tsp. fresh lemon juice

3 Granny Smith apples, peeled, sliced

2 Tbs. caramel ice cream topping or caramel apple dip

Preheat oven to 350°F. Press cookie dough into bottom of 15 × 10 × 1-inch jelly roll pan. Bake 11 to 14 minutes or until lightly browned. Cool in pan on wire rack 10 minutes. Meanwhile, mix cream cheese, sugar, peanut butter, and vanilla until well blended and smooth. Spread over cooled cookie dough. Mix water and lemon juice in small bowl. Dip apple slices in water mixture to prevent browning. Arrange apple slices on top of cream cheese mixture; drizzle with caramel topping. Cut into pieces to serve.

Apple Roll

¾ cup sugar

1 cup water

1 cup packaged biscuit mix

⅓ cup milk

1 Tbs. butter or margarine, melted

2 cups apples, diced

In a greased 8-inch square baking pan, combine sugar and water; bring to a boil. In a mixing bowl, combine biscuit mix and milk and stir until a soft dough forms. Turn dough out onto a lightly floured surface; roll or pat into a rectangle ½-inch thick and brush with melted butter. Spread apples over dough. Roll up jelly roll fashion and cut in ½-inch slices; place cut-side down in the hot syrup. Bake at 425°F for 20 minutes. Serves 6.

Apple Dumplings

DUMPLINGS
Pastry for 2 (9-inch) pie crusts
4 apples, peeled and cored
⅓ cup sugar
1 tsp. ground cinnamon
4 tsp. butter

SYRUP
1½ cups water
⅔ cup firmly packed brown sugar
2 Tbs. butter
¼ tsp. ground cinnamon

TO PREPARE DUMPLINGS: Preheat oven to 400°F. Roll out pastry on lightly floured surface. Cut out 4 (7-inch) squares. Place 1 whole apple in center of each pastry square. Mix sugar and cinnamon; spoon evenly into center of each apple. Place 1 teaspoon butter into each apple. Bring up opposite corners of pastry square to completely wrap the apple in pastry; pinch seams to seal dough. Repeat with remaining dumplings. Place dumplings in 9-inch square baking dish.

TO PREPARE SYRUP: Combine water, sugar, butter, and cinnamon in small saucepan. Bring to boil on medium-high heat, stirring constantly. Carefully pour hot syrup around dumplings in dish. Bake 40 to 45 minutes or until dumplings are golden brown.

Dutch Apple Cobbler

APPLE LAYER
1¼ cups flour
1 tsp. baking powder
1 tsp. sugar
½ cup butter
1 egg yolk
2 Tbs. milk
2½ cups apples, thinly sliced
½ cup pecans, chopped (optional)

TOPPING
¾ cup sugar
2 Tbs. butter, softened
5½ tsp. flour
¼ tsp. ground cinnamon

TO PREPARE APPLE LAYER: Preheat oven to 375°F. Mix flour, baking powder, and sugar. Cut in butter with pastry blender or 2 knives until mixture resembles coarse crumbs. Beat egg yolk and milk. Add to flour mixture; mix well. Spread batter into bottom of ungreased 8-inch square baking pan; cover with overlapping layers of apples. Sprinkle with nuts.

TO PREPARE TOPPING: Mix sugar, butter, flour, and cinnamon until well blended; sprinkle over apple mixture. Bake 30 minutes or until apples are tender. Serve warm.

Goat Cheese-Apple Dessert

6 Jonathan apples
10 oz. fresh goat cheese, softened
½ cup firmly packed brown sugar
½ cup raisins
Almonds, toasted and chopped
Whipping cream, if desired

Preheat oven to 375°F. Slice thin layer off top of each apple. Remove the core to within ½ inch of bottom. (Do not core apple all the way through.) Carefully cut out a cavity in center of each apple about 1½ inches across and 2 inches deep using paring knife. Mix goat cheese and sugar until well blended and smooth. (If the mixture is too hard to blend completely, add about ½ teaspoon lemon juice.) Stir in raisins. Spoon cheese mixture evenly into apples, mounding slightly. Smooth tops of cheese mixture; sprinkle with almonds. Place in parchment paper- or foil-lined baking dish. Bake 40 minutes. Serve hot or warm with whipping cream, if desired.

Apple Strudel

DOUGH

2 cups flour

2 Tbs. sugar

4 tsp. baking powder

½ tsp. salt

6 Tbs. cold butter or margarine

⅔ cup milk

FILLING

2½ cups Golden Delicious apples (about 2½ medium apples), finely chopped

½ cup nuts (optional)

¼ cup raisins

¼ cup packed brown sugar

2 Tbs. butter

Dash of ground cinnamon

FROSTING

1½ cups powdered sugar

2 Tbs. hot water

1 tsp. vanilla

TO PREPARE DOUGH: Preheat oven to 375°F. Mix flour, sugar, baking powder, and salt in large bowl. Cut in butter with pastry blender or 2 knives until mixture resembles coarse crumbs. Gradually stir in milk to form a soft dough. Place dough on lightly floured surface; knead gently 5 minutes. Roll out into ¼-inch-thick rectangle.

TO PREPARE FILLING: Mix apples, nuts, raisins, sugar, butter, and cinnamon; spread over dough. Roll up, jelly-roll fashion, starting at one of the short sides. Slightly bend roll into a semicircle; place on shallow greased baking pan. Bake 45 minutes.

TO PREPARE FROSTING: Meanwhile, mix powdered sugar and water until smooth. Stir in vanilla. Spread over warm strudel.

Apple-Nut Crunch

2 large eggs
1 cup firmly packed light brown sugar
½ cup flour
2 tsp. baking powder
½ tsp. salt
1 cup tart apples (1 large apple), finely chopped, peeled
1 cup pecans or walnuts, chopped
1 tsp. vanilla
½ cup whipping cream
2 tsp. granulated sugar

Preheat oven to 350°F. Beat eggs and brown sugar in large bowl with electric mixer until creamy. Mix flour, baking powder, and salt; gradually add to egg mixture, beating well after each addition. Gently stir in apples, nuts, and vanilla. Pour into greased 9-inch pie plate. Bake 30 to 35 minutes or until center is set. Cool completely on wire rack. Beat whipping cream in medium bowl with electric mixer until soft peaks form. Gradually beat in sugar; continue beating until stiff peaks form. Serve cake cut into wedges topped with a dollop of whipping cream.

Apple Snack Squares

2 eggs
2 cups sugar
¾ cup vegetable oil
2½ cups flour
1 tsp. ground cinnamon
3 cups tart apples, finely chopped, peeled
1 cup walnuts, chopped
¾ cup butterscotch chips

Preheat oven to 350°F. Mix eggs, sugar, and oil in large bowl. Stir in flour and cinnamon until well blended. (Note: Batter will be thick.) Gently stir in apples and nuts. Spread mixture into greased 13 × 9-inch baking pan; sprinkle with butterscotch chips. Bake 35 to 40 minutes or until golden brown. Cool completely in pan on wire rack. Cut into squares to serve.

PUMPKIN DESSERTS, BREADS, & MUFFINS

—— From Our Family Album ——

Alvin Eckert and his son, Curt, stand on the wagon handing bushel baskets of apples to be dumped into an apple "hopper" during apple harvest. In the 1920s, the majority of the fruit we produced was harvested for the wholesale market. All the fruit was handled in one-bushel wooden boxes. One thing has never changed, 100 percent of all the fruit we grow today is still harvested by a human hand.

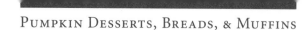

Pumpkin Smoothie

2 scoops Eckert's® Frozen Custard

½ cup extra cold milk

1 Tbs. canned pumpkin

2 tsp. brown sugar

Dash of ground cinnamon

Dash of ground nutmeg (optional)

1 tsp. vanilla yogurt or whipped topping (optional)

Colored sprinkles or dash of ground cinnamon (optional)

Add custard, milk, pumpkin, sugar, cinnamon, and nutmeg to blender; blend well until smooth. Pour into serving glass. Garnish with yogurt and sprinkles, if desired. Makes 1 serving.

Hot Buttered Drink

2¾ cups firmly packed brown sugar

1 cup unsalted butter, softened

3 Tbs. maple syrup

2 Tbs. ground cinnamon

2½ tsp. ground cloves

¾ tsp. ground nutmeg

Eckert's® Apple Cider

Mix sugar, butter, syrup, cinnamon, cloves, and nutmeg with electric mixer until well blended. Store in airtight container in refrigerator.

To serve: Stir 1½ teaspoons drink mixture into 6 ounces hot apple cider or other hot juice.

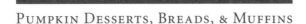
Angie's Favorite Pumpkin Bread

2 eggs
1½ cups sugar
1 cup cooked fresh or canned pumpkin
½ cup oil
1⅔ cups flour
1 tsp. baking soda
¾ tsp. salt
½ tsp. ground nutmeg
½ tsp. ground cinnamon
½ tsp. cloves
¼ tsp. ginger
¼ tsp. baking powder

Preheat oven to 350°F. Beat eggs, sugar, pumpkin, and oil with wire whisk in large bowl. Mix flour, baking soda, salt, nutmeg, cinnamon, cloves, ginger, and baking powder; stir into pumpkin mixture. Pour evenly into 2 greased 8 × 5-inch loaf pans. Bake 1 hour or until wooden toothpick inserted in center comes out clean.

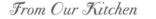

From Our Kitchen

For pumpkin muffins, line muffin cups with paper liners. Fill cup liners two-thirds full with batter. Bake 30 minutes or until toothpick inserted in center comes out clean. These muffins ship well and were often sent to the University of Illinois during final exams week.

Cream Cheese Pumpkin Muffins

FILLING

1 pkg. (8 oz.) cream cheese, softened

1 egg, beaten

2 Tbs. sugar

TOPPING

⅔ cup coconut flakes

½ cup pecans, chopped

3 Tbs. sugar

½ tsp. ground cinnamon

BATTER

2¼ cups flour

2 cups sugar

2 tsp. baking powder

2 tsp. ground cinnamon

½ tsp. salt

2 eggs, lightly beaten

1¼ cups canned pumpkin

¼ cup vegetable oil

½ tsp. vanilla

TO PREPARE FILLING: Preheat oven to 375°F. Beat egg, cream cheese, and sugar with wire whisk until well blended; set aside.

TO PREPARE TOPPING: Combine all ingredients; set aside.

TO PREPARE BATTER: Mix flour, sugar, baking powder, cinnamon, and salt in large bowl. Beat eggs, pumpkin, oil, and vanilla in small bowl with wire whisk until well blended. Add to flour mixture; stir just until moistened. Grease 24 regular-sized muffin cups or line with paper baking cups.

Fill baking cups with a heaping tablespoon of batter. Use a spoon and gently push batter to cover the bottom. Add 1 heaping teaspoonful of cream cheese filling to center of batter. Add more batter to cover the filling. Gently spread batter over filling. Each cup will be about ⅔ full. Sprinkle each with topping mixture. Bake 20 to 25 minutes or until top is golden brown. Cool in pan 5 minutes. Remove from pan to wire rack to cool. Makes 18 muffins. Store muffins in an airtight container in the refrigerator.

Pumpkin Patch Cake
with Caramel Icing

CAKE

3 eggs
1 box (18.25 oz.) spice cake mix
1 cup canned pumpkin
½ cup vegetable oil
½ cup water
1 pkg. (3 oz.) instant vanilla pudding
1 tsp. ground cinnamon
½ cup pecan pieces

ICING

¼ cup butter
½ cup firmly packed brown sugar
¼ cup milk
1¾ cups powdered sugar

TO PREPARE CAKE: Preheat oven to 350°F. Beat eggs, cake mix, pumpkin, oil, water, dry pudding mix, and cinnamon in large bowl with electric mixer on medium speed 5 minutes. Gently stir in nuts. Pour into generously buttered and floured fluted tube pan (such as a Bundt® pan). Bake 40 to 45 minutes or until wooden toothpick inserted near center of cake comes out clean. Cool in pan 15 minutes; remove to wire rack. Drizzle with caramel icing.

TO PREPARE ICING: Melt butter in small saucepan; stir in brown sugar. Bring to boil; cook 1 minute, stirring until slightly thickened. Remove from heat; cool slightly. Gradually stir in milk. Beat in powdered sugar with wire whisk until smooth. Drizzle over cake.

Apple Butter Pumpkin Pie

1 cup Eckert's® Apple Butter

1 cup puréed fresh or canned pumpkin

½ cup firmly packed brown sugar

½ tsp. salt

¾ tsp. ground cinnamon

¾ tsp. ground nutmeg

⅛ tsp. ground ginger

3 eggs, lightly beaten

¾ cup evaporated milk

1 (9-inch) unbaked pie shell

Sweetened whipping cream, for garnish

Preheat oven to 425°F. Mix apple butter, pumpkin, sugar, salt, cinnamon, nutmeg, and ginger in large bowl until mixture is well blended; stir in eggs. Gradually blend in milk; pour into pie shell and place on a sheet pan. Bake at 425°F for about 15 minutes, then lower temperature to 350°F for 40 more minutes or until center is set and a knife inserted in center comes out clean.

Garnish with whipping cream, if desired.

Traditional Pumpkin Pie

¾ cup sugar

1 tsp. ground cinnamon

½ tsp. ginger

¼ tsp. cloves

½ tsp. salt

1½ cups cooked or canned pumpkin

2 eggs, lightly beaten

1 can (14½ oz.) evaporated milk (about 1⅔ cups)

1 (9-inch) unbaked pie shell

Preheat oven to 450°F. Mix sugar, cinnamon, ginger, cloves, and salt in large bowl with wire whisk. Add pumpkin; mix well. Blend in eggs and milk. Pour into pie shell. Bake 10 minutes. Reduce oven temperature to 325°F. Bake an additional 35 minutes or until knife inserted in center comes out clean. Cool completely on wire rack.

Dutchy Pumpkin-Apple Pie

APPLE LAYER
¼ cup sugar
2 tsp. flour
½ tsp. ground cinnamon
2 apples, peeled, chopped
1 (9-inch) unbaked pie shell

FILLING
1½ cups canned pumpkin
½ cup sugar
2 Tbs. butter, melted
½ tsp. ground cinnamon
¼ tsp. ground nutmeg
¼ tsp. salt
2 eggs
1 cup evaporated milk

CRUMB TOPPING
½ cup flour
⅓ cup sugar
⅓ cup chopped nuts
3 Tbs. butter

TO PREPARE APPLE LAYER: Preheat oven to 375°F. Mix sugar, flour, and cinnamon in medium bowl. Add apples; toss to coat. Spoon into pie shell.

TO PREPARE FILLING: Mix pumpkin, sugar, butter, cinnamon, nutmeg, and salt in medium bowl with electric mixer on medium speed. Beat in eggs. Gradually blend in milk. Pour over apple mixture in pie plate. Bake 30 minutes.

TO PREPARE TOPPING: Meanwhile, combine flour, sugar, and nuts; cut in butter with pastry blender or 2 knives until mixture is crumbly. Sprinkle over pie. Bake an additional 25 to 30 minutes or until knife inserted in center comes out clean. Cool completely on wire rack. Refrigerate 3 hours before serving.

—— *From Our Kitchen* ——

Use folded pieces of foil or crust protectors to shield pie crust edges if crust becomes brown before cooking time is reached.

Fresh Pumpkin Pie

4 eggs, lightly beaten
3 cups puréed pumpkin
1 cup sugar
1½ tsp. ground cinnamon
1 tsp. ground cloves
1 tsp. ground allspice
½ tsp. ground ginger
½ tsp. salt (optional)
½ tsp. vanilla (optional)
1½ cans (12 oz. each) evaporated milk
1 (10-inch) deep dish pie shell

Preheat oven to 425°F. Beat eggs, pumpkin, sugar, cinnamon, cloves, allspice, ginger, salt, and vanilla in large bowl with electric mixer until mixture is well blended. Gradually beat in milk. Pour filling into pie shell, to within ¼-½ inch from the top of shell. Bake 15 minutes. Reduce temperature to 350°F and bake an additional 45 minutes to 1 hour or until knife inserted in center of pie comes out clean. Cool completely on wire rack. Serve topped with whipping cream, if desired.

From Our Kitchen

If you have extra pie filling, use it to make an extra, small pie with or without a crust in a ramekin or other ovenproof dish.

Pumpkin Cheese Cake

CRUST

1½ cups graham cracker crumbs
6 Tbs. margarine, melted
¼ cup sugar
½ tsp. ground cinnamon

TO PREPARE CRUST: Preheat oven to 350°F.
Mix graham cracker crumbs, margarine, sugar,
and cinnamon. Press firmly into bottom of 13
× 9-inch baking pan or 9-inch springform pan.
Bake 8 minutes.

FILLING

2 pkgs. (8 oz. each) cream cheese, softened
¾ cup sugar
2 cups cooked pumpkin
1 tsp. ground cinnamon
¼ tsp. ground nutmeg
Pinch of salt
2 eggs

TO PREPARE FILLING: Meanwhile, beat
cream cheese and sugar in large bowl with
electric mixer on medium speed. Add pumpkin,
cinnamon, nutmeg, and salt; mix well. Add eggs,
one at a time, beating just until blended after each
addition. Pour into crust. Bake 50 minutes.

Cranberry Pumpkin Cookies

½ cup butter, softened
1 cup sugar
1 cup canned pumpkin
1 egg
1 tsp. vanilla
2¼ cups flour
2 tsp. baking powder
1 tsp. baking soda
1 tsp. ground cinnamon
½ tsp. salt
1 cup fresh cranberries
1 Tbs. orange zest
½ cup walnuts, chopped

Preheat oven to 375°F. Grease baking sheets. Beat
butter and sugar in large bowl with electric mixer
on medium speed until light and fluffy. Add
pumpkin, egg, and vanilla; mix well. Combine
flour, baking powder, baking soda, cinnamon,
and salt. Add to pumpkin mixture, beating until
well blended. Gently stir in cranberries, nuts, and
zest. Drop by teaspoonfuls, 2 inches apart, onto
prepared baking sheets. Bake 10 to 12 minutes or
until cookies are set.

Easy Pumpkin Swirl

3 eggs
1 cup sugar
⅔ cup canned pumpkin
¾ cup biscuit mix
2 tsp. ground cinnamon
1 tsp. pumpkin pie spice
1 cup pecans, chopped
2 to 3 Tbs. powdered sugar

FILLING

1 pkg. (8 oz.) cream cheese, softened
⅓ cup butter, softened
1 cup powdered sugar
1 tsp. vanilla

Grease bottom and sides of 15 × 10 × 1-inch baking pan (jelly roll pan); line bottom of pan with waxed paper. Beat eggs in large bowl with electric mixer on high until thick and pale. Gradually beat in sugar, beating for 2 to 4 minutes until soft peaks form and sugar dissolves. Fold in pumpkin. In a separate bowl, combine biscuit mix and spices. Fold into pumpkin mixture and mix well. Spread evenly into prepared pan; sprinkle with chopped pecans. Bake at 375°F for 13 to 15 minutes. Sift powdered sugar in a 15 × 10-inch rectangle on a cloth towel. When cake is done, immediately loosen from sides of pan and turn out onto sugared towel; carefully peel off waxed paper. Starting at narrow end, roll up cake and towel together; cool completely on wire rack, seam-side down.

TO PREPARE FILLING: In a small bowl, beat cream cheese and butter on medium with electric mixer until creamy. Sift powdered sugar and add to mixture. Add vanilla and beat well. Unroll cake, spread with cream cheese mixture, and reroll without towel. Place on serving plate, seam-side down. Chill at least 2 hours. Serves 12.

—— *From Our Farm* ——

In preparation for the fall decorating season, we plant acres of pumpkins in mid-June from seed. Our pumpkin patch moves to a different location each year to protect the crop from soilborne diseases.

Pumpkin Bread Pudding

10 cups stale Eckert's Country White Bread, cubed
3 eggs
1½ cups milk
1 can (15 oz.) pumpkin
¾ cup firmly packed dark brown sugar
1½ tsp. ground cinnamon
2 tsp. vanilla
⅛ tsp. ground nutmeg

Preheat oven to 350°F. Layer half of the bread cubes in greased 13 × 9-inch baking dish. Mix eggs, milk, pumpkin, sugar, cinnamon, vanilla, and nutmeg with wire whisk until well blended. Pour half of the egg mixture over bread in dish. Top with remaining bread cubes; pour remaining egg mixture over bread. Press on bread to evenly moisten. Cover; refrigerate 30 minutes. Bake 45 to 50 minutes or until wooden toothpick inserted in center comes out clean. Cool slightly before serving.

Sweet Potato Bread Pudding with Streusel

BREAD PUDDING

1 lb. sweet potatoes, peeled, sliced

½ cup whipping cream

1 cup milk

2 eggs

1 cup golden raisins

¾ cup firmly packed light brown sugar

¼ cup Amaretto or rum

1 Tbs. vanilla

1 tsp. pumpkin pie spice

6 cups French or Italian bread (½-inch cubes), cubed (can be stale)

1 Tbs. butter

STREUSEL

⅓ cup flour

⅓ cup firmly packed light brown sugar

½ tsp. pumpkin pie spice

½ cup pecans, chopped

¼ cup cold unsalted butter

TO PREPARE BREAD PUDDING: Place sweet potatoes in steamer basket; steam over boiling water 20 to 30 minutes or until soft and tender. Mash potatoes with masher or put potatoes through ricer for smooth purée. Measure purée to get 1 cup. (Any extra purée can be frozen for another use.) Bring cream and milk just to boil in a small saucepan over medium heat to scald mixture. Immediately remove from heat. Beat eggs, raisins, sugar, Amaretto, vanilla, pumpkin pie spice, and the cup of sweet potato purée in large bowl with wire whisk until well blended. Gradually beat in hot cream mixture. Add bread cubes; stir gently to coat. Cover; refrigerate 30 minutes to allow bread to absorb the liquid. Meanwhile, move oven rack to lower third of oven; preheat oven to 350°F. Grease 9-inch square baking pan with butter; spoon bread mixture into pan.

TO PREPARE STREUSEL: Combine flour, sugar, pumpkin pie spice, and nuts in small bowl. Cut in butter with pastry blender or 2 knives until mixture resembles coarse crumbs. Sprinkle over bread mixture in pan. Place pan in larger baking pan. Add enough water to larger baking pan to come halfway up side of 9-inch square pan. Bake 45 minutes or until center is set and pudding is golden. Serve warm or cool completely on wire rack. Cut into squares to serve. Store leftovers in refrigerator.

Eckert's Family History

Today, the sixth and seventh generations oversee the daily operations of the Eckert farms. The current Eckert orchard business began in 1837 when Johann Peter Eckert landed in Pittsburgh, Pennsylvania, from Dietzenbach, Hesse Darmestadt, Germany, with his wife and four sons. As German tradition would have it, Johann Peter farmed and eventually bought each of his sons a farm. Johann's son Michael followed his instinctive love for the land and lived on the farm we now call Drum Hill, near Fayetteville, Illinois.

The first fruit trees were planted on Michael Eckert's farm in 1862. Michael had three children, but only one son, Henry, lived to adulthood. After his marriage in 1877, Henry built the present Eckert home on Turkey Hill in 1880. The first fruit trees were planted on Turkey Hill in 1890. Henry and Mary Eckert had three sons and a daughter, who died in infancy. Their youngest son, Alvin O., married Ella Heinrich and resided in the family home where they raised three sons, Cornell, Curt, and Vernon.

Turkey Hill Farm today is what we call our Belleville farm. The first roadside farm stand was opened on Turkey Hill by Alvin O. in 1910 and became the nucleus of our growing business. All three sons majored in agriculture at the University of Illinois and returned home after graduation to turn the business into a father-sons partnership.

Today, Jim Eckert, son of Juanita and Vernon, is president of Eckert Orchards and is the company's chief horticulturist. Lary Eckert, son of Curt and Ruth, recently resigned as president of Eckert's, Inc., after presiding over the company for 30 years. Lary's son, Chris Eckert, succeeded him as president. Chris oversees retail operations, as well as the growing and wholesaling of homegrown products. Additionally, Lary's daughter, Jill Eckert-Tantillo, is vice president of Marketing and Food Services. Angie Eckert, Chris's wife, is vice president of Retail Operations for both the Country Store and the Garden Center.

Index of Recipes